ROMANS

In this most pivotal book, Paul immediately introduces himself and his intention: "My mandate and message is to announce the goodness of God to mankind. This message is what the Scriptures are all about."

It is about what God did right, not what Adam did wrong. The good news reveals how God's righteousness rescued the life of our design and redeemed our innocence. Mankind's futile efforts to obey moral laws have failed them miserably - the Good News shifts the emphasis away from mankind's failure and condemnation to highlight what it was that God accomplished in Jesus Christ on mankind's behalf!

Behold how beautiful
how valuable
how loved
how innocent
and redeemed
you are!

In the Mirror,
Bible language becomes heart to heart
whispers of grace!

Editing: Graham Cockrell and Jane Crofts

Editing preparation for printing: Sean Osmond

Mirror Word Logo by: Wilna Furstenburg

Cover Design by: Sean Osmond

Published by Mirror Word Publishing

Should you wish to order printed copies in bulk, [2 or more] pls contact us at info@mirrorword.net

Contact us if you wish to help sponsor Mirror Bibles in Spanish, Shona or Xhosa.

Highly recommended books by the same author: Divine Embrace, God Believes in You, The Logic of His Love.

Children's books: The Eagle Story, by Lydia and Francois du Toit, illustrated by Carla Krige

Stella's Secret by Lydia du Toit and illustrated by Wendy Francisco.

The Mirror Bible, Divine Embrace God Believes in You and The Logic of His Love are also available on Kindle. The new updated Mirror Bible App is avaiable on our website

www.mirrorword.net

Subscribe to Francois facebook updates http://www.facebook.com/francois.toit

The Mirror Translation fb group http://www.facebook.com/groups/179109018883718/

ISBN 978-0-9922236-4-9

*mirror*WORD

THE MIRROR STUDY BIBLE

The Mirror Study Bible is a paraphrased translation from the Greek text. While strictly following the literal meaning of the original, sentences have been constructed so that the larger meaning is continually emphasized by means of an expanded text.

Some clarifying notes are included in italics. This is a paraphrased study rather than a literal translation. While the detailed shades of meaning of every Greek word and its components have been closely studied, this is done taking into account the consistent context of the entire chapter within the wider epistle, and bearing in mind that Jesus is what the Scriptures are all about and humankind is what Jesus is all about.

To assist the reader in their study, I have numerically superscripted the Greek word and corresponded it with the closest English word in the italicized commentary that follows. This is to create a direct comparison of words between the two languages.

I translated several Pauline epistles in the eighties
but these were never published.

In 2007 I started with the Mirror Translation. This is an ongoing process and will eventually include the entire New Testament as well as select portions of the Old Testament.

Completed books and chapters as of April 2022 are:

Luke's Gospel; John's Gospel, Romans, 1 Corinthians, 2 Corinthians,

Galatians, Ephesians, Philippians, Colossians,

1 Thessalonians, 2 Timothy, Titus, Hebrews, James, 1 Peter 1,2, 2 Peter 1

1 John 1-5,

Revelation

© Copyright Francois du Toit 2012

3

I dedicate this book to you.
As you ponder these pages,
I pray, that Holy Spirit quicken
your spirit with fresh insight
and resonance
as you engage in the wonder of your
authentic innocence redeemed
in the Romance of the Ages!

Jesus is God's language and message to mankind.
He is the context of Scripture.
There is no perfect translation,
there is only a perfect Word: the Logic of God.
The Bible is all about Jesus.
What makes the book irresistibly relevant, is the fact that
Jesus is all about you!

God has found a face in you that portrays him
more beautifully than the best theology!
Your features, your touch, the cadence of your voice,
the compassion in your gaze, the lines of your smile,
the warmth of your person and presence unveil him!

INDEX

ENDORSEMENTS

Reflecting on any translation of Scripture gives one the opportunity to hear our Maker's voice and thoughts, filtered through the interpretation and language of the translator(s).
In this fresh Paraphrase, Francois du Toit has opened the curtain for readers of any age, culture or language to enjoy amazing insights into the heartbeat of *Agape* - where everyone feels equally loved, included and valued in the eyes of the Father - and fully redeemed in the union we come from!

Archbishop **DESMOND TUTU** - *Legacy Foundation*

The Mirror Bible is a transforming paraphrased translation that is simplistic, accurate, detailed and comprehensive, captivating and at the same time exuding intriguing spiritual revelation; it is divinely insightful and contemporary.

It's a must read, a befitting guide and manual for all age groups for; Bible study, meditation, devotion, worship, teaching, instruction and scholarship.

Jesus Christ is the epicenter of the entire text.

Believers will not miss the centrality of the translation as there is a finite and delicate thread directing to the revealing and redeeming Christ.

Unbelievers will derive unrivalled comfort from the text as they get captivated by the reality and close proximity of Christ.

This is definitely a life giving and transforming translation. I am humbly convinced that Francois is chosen by God to serve this generation and the next with undiluted truth in the midst of incomprehensible compromises of worldly, heretical and traditional, doctrinal interpretations and practices (religion) that have diverted us from the truth.

The Mirror Bible is a welcome revelatory and revolutionary development that is divinely sanctioned, inspired and directed. This translation is by no doubt a compelling grounding expository of our century.

Rev. **ANOUYA ANDREW MUCHECHETERE**, *MBA, MA,*
Former Secretary General of the Evangelical Fellowship of Zimbabwe (EFZ).

The mystery concerning God's Own action in Christ, balanced with the nature and necessity of our human response has defined my personal journey for many years.
When I was introduced to Francois du Toit and the Mirror Bible, much of that mystery were resolved.

6

ENDORSEMENTS

Often, I found myself 'gasping for breath' as some new aspect of the mystery of Christ and His Kingdom emerged with startling clarity. Francois' love for the text, his sheer exegetical courage and his astonishing ability to express essential biblical pre-suppositions in the intimate Love language of God, has opened for Judith and me a renewed and transformative biblical understanding.

BOB and **JUDITH MUMFORD** - www.lifechangers.org

The Mirror Translation is astonishingly beautiful. The union theme is outstanding.

The early followers of Jesus knew that he was the center of all creation, the plan from the beginning, the alpha and the omega, the author and finisher of faith. They wrestled deeply with these questions and the staggering implications of Jesus' very identity. They handed down clear and powerful and very relevant insights and answers. Francois has met the Jesus of the Apostles, and through his wrestling with their light, is providing for us all a paraphrase of their work that is as thrilling as it is beautiful and true.

My imagination ignites reading your translation. What a beautiful, breathtaking translation. This is brilliant, and destined to relieve and liberate many. You sing the Father's heart, my brother. May the Holy Spirit continue to use the Mirror to reveal Jesus and his Father and us all around this world! I love it.

DR. C. BAXTER KRUGER
Author of "The Great Dance" and "The Shack Revisited"

See your identity clearly portrayed here in The MIRROR! Exhilarating, thrilling, breathtaking beauty overtakes you in this glorious translation. God's empowering, everlasting, all-compassing Gospel of Grace – Christ's Finished Work – is here revealed in depths and dimensions of joy that will rock your world.

You are co-revealed in Christ! Co-crucified, co-included in His death and resurrection, co-buried, co-quickened, co- alive, co-seated "with Him in His executive authority in the Throne Room of the heavenly realm" (Eph. 2:5,6 The Mirror). Herewith, my highest recommendation for this new, powerful, mega-encouraging Bible translation, so rich with fresh, wide vistas of the mystery of our restored innocence in Christ.

May The MIRROR STUDY BIBLE soon be treasured in every home, seminary and School of Ministry in the world!

REV. LANI LANGLAIS - San Francisco, California

ENDORSEMENTS

The Bible is God's amazing conversation with us. Here we engage with God's words that crescendo in the revelation of his Son, Jesus Christ. The greatest joy is to realize that you as an individual are included in this conversation.

This translation is in all probability one of the greatest contributions in the last few years to the broader church. It is imperative that every Christ follower discovers their true identity mirrored in Jesus. The most liberating revelation is the fact that we have not only died together with Him, but that we were also raised with Him in resurrection life. Then to grasp that we are seated with Him in heavenly places, where we may now live our daily lives from a position of significance and influence within this world. The premise of the Good News of the Gospel is that we are not required to strive to attain something through personal achievement, but rather to discover who we already are and what we already have in Christ, as revealed in the glorious Scriptures.

May The Mirror Translation impact your life as much as it has mine, and may it facilitate your spiritual journey to truly relocate your mind, living from the new vantage point of this glorious life in Christ.

ALAN Platt - *Visionary leader of **Doxa Deo** International*

My philosophy in doing the Mirror Bible is reflected in the following example:

I do not read music, but have often witnessed our son, Stefan, approach a new piece on the piano.

His eyes see so much more than mere marks scribbled on a page;

he hears the music.

His trained mind engages even the subtleties and the nuances of the original composition, and is able to repeat the authentic sound,

knowing that the destiny of the music would never be reduced to the page;

but is always in the next moment,

where the same intended beauty is heard, and repeated again!

The best translation would always be the incarnation!

I so value the enormity of the revelation of the incarnation.

Yet, before flesh, the Word was πρoς

face to face with God!

And fragile text

scribbled through the ages in memoirs of stone, parchment and papyrus pages

carrying eternity in thought

and continues to translate faith

to faith!

Now we have the same spirit of faith as he encountered when he wrote...

"I believe

and so I speak!"

Conversation ignites!

Did not our hearts burn within our being when He spoke familiar text of ancient times, in the voices of Moses and the prophets and David and Abraham,

who saw his day

and announced its dawn in our hearts!

The mystery that was hidden for ages and generations

is now revealed!

MY PHILOSOPHY

In dealing daily with ancient text,

rediscovering thoughts buried in time, I am often overwhelmed and awed at the magnificence of eternity captured in little time capsules,

opening vistas of beauty beyond our imagination -

face to face with the same face to faceness of the Logos

and God

and us - conceived in their dream!

And irresistibly intrigued by the invitation to come and drink -

to taste and see -

from the source -

and to hear a saint reminiscing and reminding himself of the utterance of another earth dweller-brother, David, who wrote a song 3000 years ago,

"Return to your rest oh my soul!

For the Lord has dealt bountifully with you!

I believe and so I speak!"

And with fresh wounds bleeding from the many angry blows he was dealt with, Paul echoes,

"We have the same spirit of faith as he had who wrote, 'I believe and so I speak!' We too believe and so we speak!"

Let's celebrate the "sameness" of Jesus

yesterday - yes, as far as history and beyond time can go -

and today! This very finite, fragile moment -

plus the infinite future!

Inexhaustible, beyond boundaries and the confines of space and time!

INTRODUCTION TO ROMANS

ROMANS REVEALED

The Eagle Story

During our honeymoon in January, 1979, in the Blyderiver Canyons in Mpumalanga, South Africa, Lydia and I met a nature conservation officer who told us of a fascinating incident when they released a Black Eagle just the previous week; this bird, with a wingspan of more than two meters, had been in the Pretoria Zoo for ten years! She told us how excited they were when the eagle finally arrived in its wooden crate. This was the day for its release! But their excitement soon turned to frustration when, after opening the cage, the bird refused to fly. Ten years of caged life seemed to have trapped its mind in an invisible enclosure. How could they get the eagle to realize that it was indeed free? No amount of prompting and prodding seemed to help. Then, after some hours the bird suddenly looked up, and in the distance they heard the call of another eagle; immediately the zoo-eagle took off in flight!

This dramatic story left a deep impression on my mind. I knew that in the light of Paul's revelation of the Good News, we are left with one urgent priority, which is to announce to the nations with bold confidence the truth about their original identity and mirror-reflect the integrity of their redeemed innocence. No flying lessons are required when truth is realized!

This gives such clarity and content to the fact that Jesus came to the planet not to upgrade the cage of Judaism or any other religion by starting a new one called Christianity; but to be the incarnate voice of the likeness and image of God in human form! He came to reveal and redeem the image of God in us! His mission was to mirror the blueprint of our design, not as an example for us but of us! (Col 1:15, 2:9, 10).

In God's faith mankind is associated in Christ even before the foundation of the world. Jesus died mankind's death and when the stone was rolled away, we were raised together with him! Every human life is fully represented in him (Hosea 6:2).

If the gospel is not the voice of the free eagle, it is not the gospel.

Paul's Gospel

In this pivotal book, Paul immediately introduces himself and his intention: "My mandate and message is to announce the goodness of God to mankind. This message is what the Scriptures are all about. It remains the central prophetic theme and content of inspired writing." (Rom 1:1, 2).

Scripture could never again be interpreted in any other way! The good news of the success of the Cross gives content and context to Scripture.

There is nothing to be ashamed of; this message unveils how God got it right to rescue man from the effect of what Adam did wrong! (Rom 1:16, 17)

The dynamic of the gospel is the revelation of God's faith as the only valid basis of our belief (from faith to faith). Paul quotes Habakkuk who prophetically introduced a new era when he realized that righteousness would be founded in what God believes about the redeemed life of our design, and not in our clumsy attempts to be righteous.

From now on righteousness by God's faith defines life! (Hab 2:4, Rom 1:17, 3:27).

Instead of reading the curse when disaster strikes, Habakkuk realizes that the Promise out-dates performance as the basis to mankind's acquittal! Deuteronomy 28 would no longer be the motivation or the measure of right or wrong behavior! "Though the fig trees do not blossom, nor fruit be on the vines, the produce of the olive fail and the fields yield no food, the flock be cut off from the fold and there be no herd in the stalls, yet I will rejoice in the Lord, I will joy in the God of my salvation. God, the Lord, is my strength; he makes my feet like hinds' feet, he makes me tread upon my high places." (Hab 3:17-19 RSV).

From Romans chapters 1:18 to 3:20, Paul proceeds to give a graphic display of distorted human behavior as a result of suppressing the truth of their redeemed innocence and likeness.

Rom 1:18 God is not standing neutral to mankind's indifference. This revelation of God's belief in our redeemed righteousness is at the same time an unveiling of God's passionate desire, from a heavenly perspective, towards a humanity who seemed to have lost touch with the romance of their devotion by suppressing the truth about themselves; they have forgotten the delicate art to adore and be adored; while they continue to hold on to an inferior reference of themselves by being out of sync with their true likeness! Rom 1:19 God is not a stranger to anyone; whatever can be known of God is manifest in man. God has revealed it in the very core of their being which bears witness within their own conscience!

Being a Jew, and therefore to be acquainted with the requirements of the law, offers no real advantage, since it offers no disguise or defense from sin. It bears the same symptoms and consequences. His triumphant statement in verses 16, 17 of chapter 1 and again reinforced in chapter 3:21-24, is set against this backdrop. The good news declares how the same condemned mankind in Adam is now freely acquitted by God's grace through the redemption that is unveiled in Christ Jesus.

He brings the argument of the ineffectiveness of the law to get a person to change their behavior, to a final crescendo in Chapter 7. He states in 7:1 that he is writing to those who know the law. They have first-hand experience therefore of the weakness of the rule to consistently govern a person's conduct.

The best the law could offer was to educate and confirm good intention; but the more powerful law, the law of sin introduced to mankind through one man's transgression, has to be challenged by a greater force than human willpower.

Because sin robbed mankind of their true identity and awakened in them all kinds of worse-than-animal-like conduct, a set of rules couldn't do it. The revelation of God's righteousness has to be far more effective and powerful than mankind's slavery to sin.

In the typical language of the law, mankind's corrupt behavior deserves nothing less than condemnation. Yet within this context the grace and mercy of God is revealed; not as mere tolerance from God's side to turn a blind eye and to put up with sin, but as God's triumphant act in Christ to cancel our guilt and to break sin's spell and dominion over us.

For salvation to be relevant it has to offer mankind a basis and reference from which their faith is to be launched. It has to offer a conclusion of greater implication than the stalemate condition they find themselves in under the dispensation of the law.

"My inner person agrees that the law is good and desires to obey its requirements yet my best intentions leave me powerless against the demands of sin in my body! Oh, wretched being that I am!"

Woe be to us but for the revelation of God's righteous intervention! The man Christ Jesus is the mediator of mankind. The judgment mankind rightfully deserved fell on him; he was made to be sin who knew no sin. "He was handed over because of our transgressions, and triumphantly raised because of our acquittal." (Rom 4:25).

Paul is convinced that whatever happened to the human race because of Adam's fall is far superseded in every possible proportion by the revelation of mankind's inclusion in the life, death and resurrection of Jesus Christ. He places the fall of Adam and every act of unrighteousness that followed against the one act of righteousness that God performed in Christ as proof of mankind's acquittal.

The revelation of righteousness by God's faith unveils how Jesus Christ represented and redeemed mankind. The etymological essence of the word, "righteousness" in its stem, diké, implies the idea of two parties finding likeness in each other; with no interference of any sense of blame, guilt or inferiority. The Hebrew word for righteousness is the word *tzedek,* צדק which also includes the idea of the wooden beam in a scale of balances. When Adam lost the glory of God (Hebrew, כבוד

kabod, weight; the consciousness of God's likeness and image) the law proved that no amount of good works could balance the scale again. Grace reveals how God redeemed his image and likeness again in human form; now the scale is perfectly balanced! No wonder Jesus cried out on the cross, "It is finished!" *See commentary note on 2 Corinthians 6:14.*

This is the message that Paul says he owes to the entire world!

"I proclaim Jesus Christ according to the revelation of the mystery which was concealed in silence in the sequence of timeless ages, but now is made publicly known, mirrored in prophetic Scripture." ("Surely he was wounded by our transgressions; he was bruised by our iniquities. The chastisement that brought us peace was upon him and by his stripes we were healed." [Isa 53:4, 5]) And now the God of the ages has issued his mandate to make the mystery known in such a way that all the nations of the earth will discover the lifestyle that the hearing of faith ignites." (Rom 16:25, 26) Paul gives new definition to obedience when he calls it "the obedience of faith." Romans 1:5.

"The conclusion is clear: it took just one offence to condemn mankind; one act of righteousness declares the same mankind innocent. The disobedience of the one exhibits mankind as sinners, the obedience of another exhibits mankind as righteous. Romans 5:18, 19.

Just as all mankind became exceedingly sinful through one person's disobedience but did not know it until the law revealed it, so all mankind became exceedingly righteous through one act of righteousness but they do not know it until the gospel reveals it. The principle of faith is to see what God sees. God calls things that seem not to be as though they were. Romans 4:17.

While we look not at the things that the senses observe, we look at the revelation of the unseen as it is unveiled in our understanding through the mirror revelation of the Gospel of Christ. See 2 Corinthians 3:18; 2 Corinthians 4:18.

Romans 4:17 finds its context in Romans 1:17 and 10:17, "It is clear then that faith's source is found in the content of the message heard; the message is Christ. (We are God's audience; Jesus is God's language!)"

The incarnation is the voice of the free eagle.

(The beautifully illustrated Eagle Story is available on Amazon.)

1:1 Paul, [5]passionately engaged by Jesus Christ, [1]identified in him to [2]represent him. My [3]mandate and [4]message is to announce the goodness of God to mankind. *(Mandate, the scope or horizon of my message, from [3]**horitso**, meaning marked out. The word, [2]**apostelo**, means an extension from him, a representative; [5]**doulos**, means slave from **deo**, to be bound or knitted together like a husband and wife; [1]**kletos** comes from **kaleo**, meaning called, to identify by name, to surname; and [4]**eu + angellion**, means well done announcement, good news, the official announcement of God's goodness.)*

1:2 This message is what the Scriptures are all about. It remains the central prophetic theme and content of inspired writing.

1:3 The Son of God has his natural lineage from the seed of David; *(In Matthew 22:41-45 Jesus asked the Pharisees, "What do you think of the Christ? Whose son is he?" They said to him, "The son of David." He said to them, "How is it then that David, inspired by the Spirit, calls him Lord, saying, 'The Lord said to my Lord, Sit at my right hand, till I put your enemies under your feet'? If David thus calls him Lord, how is he his son?" Mat 22:41-45 "You must not call anyone here on earth Father, because you have only the one Father in heaven." [Mt 23:9]. "Yet there is for us only one God, the Father, who is the Creator of all things and for whom we live; and there is only one Lord, Jesus Christ, through whom all things were created and through whom we live." [1 Cor 8:6]. "For this reason I bow my knees before the Father, from whom every family in heaven and on earth receives its true name." [Eph 3:14, 15]. "... there is one God and Father of all people, who is Lord of all, works through all, and is in all." [Eph 4:6, 7].)*

1:4 however, his powerful resurrection from the dead by the Holy Spirit, [1]locates and confirms his being and sonship in God. *(The word translated, locates, comes from [1]**apo + horizo**, meaning to mark out beforehand, to define or locate; literally, horizon. The same word is translated as mandate in verse 1. In Acts 13:32-33, Paul preaches the resurrection and quotes Psalms 2, "Today I have begotten you." Jesus locates us and confirms that we have our genesis in God! Peter understands that we were born anew in the resurrection of Christ. The relevance of the resurrection is the revelation of mankind's inclusion in Christ [see 1 Pet 1:3]. Hosea 6:2 is the only Scripture that prophesies the third day resurrection, and here in this single dramatic prophesy, we are co-included in his resurrection! "After two days he will revive us, on the third day he will raise us up!" [RSV] This is the crux of the mystery of the Gospel! "Will the earth be brought forth in one day? Can a nation be born in a moment?" [Isa 66:8, 9].)*

1:5 The grace and commission we received from him, is to bring about a [1]faith-inspired lifestyle in all the nations. [2]His name is his claim on the human race. *(Paul immediately sets out to give new definition to the term, "obedience," no longer by law, but of faith. [1]Obedience,* *from **upo** + **akoo**, means to be under the influence of what is heard, accurate hearing; hearing from above. ²Every family in heaven and on earth is identified in him. Eph 3:15.)*

1:6 In Jesus Christ you individually discover ¹who you are. *(The word, ¹kaleo, means to call by name, to surname.)*

1:7 In addressing you, I address all in Rome. I am convinced of God's love for you; he ²restored you to the harmony of your original design; you were made holy in Christ Jesus; no wonder then that you are ¹surnamed ²Saints. His grace gift in Christ secures your total wellbeing. The Father of the Lord Jesus Christ is ours also; he is our God. *(The word, ¹kaleo, means called, identified by name, surname; ²hagios, means saints, restored to the harmony of your original design; "He separated me from my mother's womb when he revealed his Son in me, in order that I may declare him in the nations; immediately I did not consult with flesh and blood." [Gal 1:15, 16]. "From now on, therefore, we regard no one from a human point of view; even though we once knew Christ after the flesh, we regard him thus no longer." [2 Cor 5:16 RSV].)*

1:8 My greatest joy is to realize that your faith is announced throughout the entire world. The total ¹cosmos is our audience. *(The word, kosmos in the NT refers to the entire human family.)*

1:9 I am completely engaged in my spirit in the gospel of God's Son; constantly including you in my prayers; God is my witness.

1:10 Since I already feel so ¹connected to you I long to also see you face to face. *(¹To beseech, deomai, from deo to tie together, to be knitted together.)*

1:11 I really look forward to finally meet you in person, knowing that my spiritual ¹gift will benefit you greatly; it will cement and establish you in your faith. *(The word, ¹metadidomi, translates as the kind of giving where the giver is not distanced from the gift but wrapped up in it! The Apostles, Prophets, preachers, pastors, and teachers are gifts to the ekklesia to establish them in their faith and to present everyone in the full and mature stature of Christ [Eph 4:11-16]. There is such a vast difference between a gift and a reward! We are God's gifts to one another. What God now has in us is gift wrapped to the world. What we are in our individual expression is a gift and not a reward for personal diligence or achievement. These gifts were never meant to establish one above the other, or to become mere formal titles, but rather to identify specific and dynamic functions with one defined purpose, to bring everyone into the realization of the fullness of the measure of Christ in them!)*

1:12 And so we will be mutually refreshed in the ¹participation and reflection of our common faith. *(The word, ¹sumparakaleo, comes from sum, together; para, is a Preposition indicating close proximity,* *a thing proceeding from a sphere of influence, with a suggestion of union of place of residence, to have sprung from its author and giver, originating from, denoting the point from which an action originates, intimate connection, and **kaleo**, meaning to identify by name, to surname.)*

1:13 Until now I have been prevented from coming to you, even though I have frequently desired to reap some harvest in you as much as I anticipate the full fruit of this gospel in all the nations.

1:14 I am so convinced of everyone's inclusion; I am [2]indebted both to the Greeks as well as those many [1]foreigners whose languages we do not even understand. I owe this message to everyone, it is not a matter of how literate and educated people are; the illiterate are equally included in the benefit of the Good News. *(The word, [1]bar-baros, means one who speaks a strange and foreign language; [2]opheiletes, means to be indebted, obliges one to return something to someone that belongs to him or her in the first place.)*

1:15 Because of this compelling urgency I am so keen to preach to you Romans also.

1:16 I have no shame about sharing the Good News of Christ with anyone; the powerful rescuing act of God persuades both Jew and Gentile alike.

1:17 Herein lies the secret of the power of the Gospel; there is no good news in it until the righteousness of God is revealed. The dynamic of the gospel is the revelation of [1]God's faith as the only valid basis for our belief. The Prophets wrote in advance about the fact that God believes that righteousness reveals the life of our design. "Righteousness by his *(God's)* **faith defines life."** *(In David's dramatic, prophetic account of the crucifixion in Psalm 22, he concludes with verse 27, "All the ends of the earth shall remember and return to the Lord; and all the families of the nations shall worship before him." And in verse 31, "...they shall declare his righteousness to a people that shall yet be born; that he has done it." The gospel is the revelation of the righteousness of God; it unveils how the Father, Son and Spirit succeeded to put mankind right with themselves. It is about what God did right, not what Adam did wrong. The good news reveals how God's righteousness rescued the life of our design and redeemed our innocence. Mankind's futile efforts to justify themselves, have failed them miserably. [Rom 7] The Good News shifts the emphasis away from our failure and condemnation to highlight what it was that God accomplished in Jesus Christ on humanity's behalf. "Look away [from the law of works] unto Jesus; he is the [1]Author and finisher of faith." [Hebrews 12:2]. It is God's faith to begin with; it is **[1]from faith to faith**, and not our good or bad behavior; we are not defined by our performance or circumstances.*

*The Greek word translated "from" is the Preposition, ¹**ek**, which always denotes source or origin. The language of the old written code was, "Do in order to become. The language of the new is, "Be, because of what was done." Instead of do, do, do, it's done, done, done. Paul refers here to Habakkuk 2:4, "The just shall live by his [God's] faith." Habakkuk sees a complete new basis to mankind's standing before God. Instead of reading the curse when disaster strikes, he realizes that the Promise out-dates performance as the basis to mankind's acquittal. The curse is taken out of the equation. Galatians 3:13. Deuteronomy 28 would no longer be the motivation or measure of right or wrong behavior. Instead of righteousness as a reward to mankind's efforts to obey the law, Habakkuk celebrates God's righteousness based on God's belief, in the face of apparent disaster, represented in the evidence of all the curses mentioned in Deut 28. He sings, "Though the fig trees do not blossom, nor fruit be on the vines, the produce of the olive fails and the fields yield no food, the flock be cut off from the fold and there be no herd in the stalls, yet I will rejoice in the Lord, I will joy in the God of my salvation. God, the Lord, is my strength; he makes my feet like hinds' feet, he makes me tread upon my high places." [Habakkuk 3:17-19 RSV]. It is interesting to note that Habakkuk - חבקוק **chǎbaqûq**, was possibly the son of the Shunammite woman and her husband who hosted the Prophet Elisha. They could not have children, until Elisha declared that in a year's time she would embrace - חבק **chabaq** - a child. When the child grew up to be a young man he died of sunstroke and Elisha stretched himself over the boy and mirror-embraced the dead child, face to face and the boy came back to life. חבקוק **Chabaquq** is a double embrace - it is the prophetic picture of our mirror-resurrection together with Christ. If anyone knew that righteousness was not by works, but by God's faith, it was Habakkuk.*

*The word righteousness comes from the Anglo Saxon word, "rightwiseness;" wise in that which is right. In Greek the word for righteousness is **dikaiosune**, from **dikay**, that which is right; it is a relationship word and refers to two parties finding likeness in each other. Righteousness points to harmony in a relationship. See 2 Corinthians 6:14. Faith-righteousness has nothing in common with the pagan philosophies of karma and performance-based approval; they could never balance the scales or be evenly yoked together in any context. [The word **heterozugeō**, an unequal or different yoke; from the Hebrew word, **zugot**, זוגות indicates pairs of two identical objects; a yoke or a teaching; the yoke of a rabbi or philosopher represented their doctrine; reminds of the Hebrew word for righteousness, **tzedek**, צדק which also includes the idea of the wooden beam in a scale of balances. "He that judges his neighbor according to the balance of righteousness, or innocence, they judge him according to righteousness." [T. Bab. Sabbat, fol. 127. 2.]*

*It is interesting to note that the Greek goddess of Justice is Dike, [pronounced, **dikay** - the stem of the word **dikaiosune**, righteousness] and she is always pictured holding a scale of balances in her hand. See also 2 Corinthians 6:15. In Colossians 2:9-10, "It is in Christ that God finds an accurate and complete expression of himself, in a human body. He mirrors our completeness and is the ultimate authority of our true identity.")*

1:18 God is not standing neutral to mankind's indifference. This revelation of God's belief in our redeemed righteousness is at the same time an unveiling of God's [1]passionate desire, from a heavenly perspective, [2]towards a [3]humanity who seemed to have [5]lost touch with the romance of their devotion by [4]suppressing the truth about themselves; they have [5]forgotten the delicate art to adore and be adored; while they continue to hold on to an [6]inferior reference of themselves by being out of sync with their true likeness! *(God's belief in mankind's redeemed righteousness is endorsed in the heavens and in sharp contrast to the counterfeit, earthly reference that blindfolds people in their own unrighteousness. The word often translated wrath, [1]**orge**, means desire - as a reaching forth or excitement of the mind, passion. The Preposition [2]**epi** means towards, continuous influence upon; I interpreted it here as "contrast". The word for the [3]human species, male or female is **anthropos**, from **ana**, upward, and **tropos**, manner of life; character; in like manner. The word [4]**katecho**, to echo downwards is the opposite of **anoche**, to echo upward; see Romans 2:4 and 3:26. In Colossians 3:2 Paul encourages us to engage our thoughts with things above [God's belief], and not below [law of works]. The word, ασεβειαν [5]**asebeian**, from **a**, negative and **sebomai**, to adore, to worship. The word [6]**adikia**, unrighteousness, is the opposite of **dikay**, two parties finding likeness in each other; thus, to be out of sync with likeness. The law reveals how guilty and sinful mankind is, while the gospel reveals how forgiven and restored to their original blueprint we are. See 2 Corinthians 4:4.)*

1:19 God is not a stranger to anyone; whatever can be known of God is [1]manifest in man. God has revealed it in the very core of their being which bears witness within their own conscience! *(Note Rom 2:14 & 15 For even a pagan's natural instinct will confirm the law to be present in their conscience and though they have never even heard about Jewish laws. Thus they prove to be a law unto themselves. The law is so much more than a mere written code; its presence in human conscience even in the absence of the written instruction is obvious. See also 2 Corinthians 4:4 & 7 and Colossians 1:27. Blindfold-mode does not remove the treasure from where it was hidden all along! Every time we love, encounter joy, or experience beauty, a hint of the nature of our Maker reflects within us; even in the experience of the unbeliever. In the incarnation Jesus unveils God's likeness, not his "otherness", in human form as in a mirror! The word [1]**phaneros** from **phaino**, means to shine like light. Colossians 2:9,10 "It is in Christ that God finds an accurate and complete expression of himself, in a human body! Jesus mirrors our completeness." While the expanse cannot measure or define*

God, his exact likeness is displayed in human form. Jesus proves that human life is tailor-made for God! See also Ephesians 4:8 And James 3:9 We can say beautiful things about God the Father but with the same mouth curse a fellow human made in his mirror likeness. The point is not what the person did to deserve the insult! The point is that people are image and likeness bearers of God by design!)

1:20 God is on display in creation; the very fabric of visible cosmos appeals to reason. It clearly bears witness to the ever present sustaining power and intelligence of the invisible God, leaving mankind without any valid excuse to ignore him. *(Psalm 19:1-4, "God's glory is on tour in the skies, God-craft on exhibit across the horizon. Madame Day holds classes every morning, Professor Night lectures each evening. Their words aren't heard, their voices aren't recorded, But their silence fills the earth: unspoken truth is spoken everywhere." — The Message.)*

1:21 Yet mankind only knew him in a philosophical religious way, from a distance, and failed to give him credit as God. Their taking him for granted and lack of gratitude veiled him from them; they became absorbed in useless debates and discussions, which further darkened their understanding about themselves.

1:22 Their wise conclusions only confirmed their folly.

1:23 Their losing sight of God, made them lose sight of who they really were. In their calculation the image and likeness of God became reduced to a corrupted and distorted pattern of themselves. Suddenly a person has more in common with "creepy crawlies" than with their original blueprint.

1:24 It seemed like God abandoned mankind to be swept along by the lusts of their own hearts to abuse and defile themselves. Their most personal possession, their own bodies, became worthless public property.

1:25 Truth suppressed *(v18)* **became twisted truth. Instead of embracing their Maker as their authentic identity, they preferred the deception of a distorted image of their own making, religiously giving it their affection and worship. The true God is the blessed God of the ages. Hey! He is not defined by our devotion or indifference!** *(And all this because they traded the true God for a fake god, and worshiped the god they made instead of the God who made them. Message.)*

1:26 By being confused about their Maker they became confused about themselves; which led to all manner of obsessions.

1:27 Men and women alike became inflamed with perverted fantasies. This brought about an intense [1]striving and a [2]most exhausting toiling in the pursuit of a [3]disillusioned identity - which clearly are the symptoms of an [4]inferior estimate of oneself. *(The word, [1]orexei* *describes a reaching out after something. The word [2]katergazomai from kata, downward; also to emphasize intensity; and ergatsomai, to toil. Then he uses the word [3]aschēmosunē from aschēmōn, deformed, from a, negative or without and schema, form or pattern. The word [4]antimisthia from anti, against or opposite and misthois, the wage of a hireling; translated here an inferior estimate; or a wage that leaves one disappointed. This word is only used again in 2 Corinthians 6:13.)*

1:28 Their indifference to their god-identity, veiled God from them.

1:29 Sin snowballs! It spreads like a disease, exhibiting its ugly symptoms in every possible form, from perverse sexual obsessions, to every kind of atrocity. The problem with sin is that it never satisfies, leaving the victim miserably unfulfilled and constantly craving for more of the same deception: vileness, jealousy, anger and an unnatural obsession with self. Life is cheap, murder doesn't matter; they are steeped in constant quarrelling and wickedness, their conversation has become reduced to slanderous gossip.

1:30 No one is safe in their company; they think that by insulting people they can voice their hatred for God; proudly bragging about their latest inventions of filth. They remain [1]indifferent to any definition of [2]parenthood, disregarding the fact that we did not invent ourselves. *(The word [1]apeithēs, where we get the word apathy from, traditionally translated to disobey, in my opinion translates better as being indifferent; from a, negative and peithō, to believe; to make friends, to win one's favor, gain one's good will, or to strive to please one. The word [2]goneus, parent; from ginomai, to be born.)*

1:31 They live [1]dysfunctional, [2]disconnected lives where no [3]sympathy or mercy is shown. *(The words, [1]asynetous, a, negative and sunetos; from suniemi; a joining together like that of two streams; a fusion of thought, a joint-seeing. Thus, with them, there seems to be no compatibility or harmony to connect meaningfully with others. The word [2]asunthetos again, a, negative and suntithemai - to stand in agreement or support with of another. They live completely out of sync with others. Then Paul uses the words, [3]astorgos, without natural affection and eleēmōn, no mercy.)*

1:32 It just doesn't make any sense, they started off knowing the [1]righteousness of God, yet by their lifestyle they flirt with death; it is almost as if sin has become a fashionable contest. *([1]dikaioma, righteousness - not judgment, as some translations suggest!)*

From verse 18 to 32 Paul paints the picture of the dilemma and darkness of the fallen mindset - where the distorted picture becomes the norm. This is the language of a law system, which defines people by their behavior rather than their design. He then concludes in 2:4 with this amazing statement to underline his conviction as recorded in 1:16,17 about the powerful rescuing act of God announced in the Gospel. "Do not underestimate God's kindness. The wealth of his benevolence and his resolute refusal to let go of us is because he continues to hear the echo of his likeness in us! Thus his patient passion is to shepherd everyone into a radical mind shift.)

2:1 A presumed knowledge of that which is right or wrong does not qualify you to judge anyone; especially if you do exactly the same stuff you notice other people do wrong. You effectively condemn yourself. No one is another person's judge.

2:2 God must judge all transgression, but your judging others does not make them any guiltier.

2:3 God is completely impartial in his judgment; you are not scoring any points or disguising your own sins by telling on others.

2:4 Do not [1]underestimate God's [2]kindness. The wealth of his [2]benevolence and his [3]resolute refusal to let go of us is because he continues to hear the echo of his likeness in us! Thus his [4]patient passion is to [5]shepherd everyone into a [6]radical mind shift. *(The word translated, underestimate is the word, [1]kataphroneō, from kata, down, and phroneo, to think, to form an opinion; thus a downcast mind, to despise or take for granted. It is the revelation of the goodness of God that leads us to [6]repentance; it is not our "repentance" that leads God to goodness! The word "repentance" is a fabricated word from the Latin word, paenitentia, which became penance, and to give religion more mileage the English word became re-penance! That is not what the Greek word means at all! The word, [6]metanoia, comes from meta, together with and noieō, to perceive with the mind. It describes the awakening of the mind to that which is true; a re-alignment of one's reasoning; it is a gathering of one's thoughts, a co-knowing. Faith is not a decision; it is a discovery. [See Isa 55:8-10] The word, [2]chrestos, kind, benevolent, from xeir, hand which is also connected to the word xristos, to draw the hand over, to anoint, to measure; see also the Hebrew for Messiah, משיח to anoint; to measure, from mashach, משח to draw the hand over, to measure! [Analytical Hebrew and Chaldee Lexicon, B Davidson.] In Jesus Christ, God has measured mankind innocent, he is the blueprint of our design! The word [3]anoches comes from ana, meaning upward; ana also shows intensity and the word echo, to hold, or embrace, as in echo. He continues to hear the echo of his likeness in us! [See Rom 3:26.] The word, [4]makrothumias, means to be patient in bearing the offenses and injuries of others. Literally, passion that goes a long way; from the stem thuo, to slay a sacrifice. The word, [5]ago, means to lead as a shepherd leads his sheep.)*

2:5 A calloused heart that resists change accumulates cause to self-destruction, while God's righteous judgment is revealed in broad daylight. *(The gospel openly reveals that God declared mankind innocent.)*

2:6 By resisting him you are on your own; your own deeds will judge you. *(Rejecting his goodness [v 4] keeps you snared in a lifestyle ruled by sin-consciousness and condemnation.)*

2:7 The quest of mankind is to be [1]constant in expressing that which is good and glorious and of imperishable value. We are eager to engage the original blueprint-life of the [2]ages. *(The word, ὑπομονή [1]hupomone - to continue to be present; consciously abiding undisturbed in seamless union with your Source.*

The life of the ages, from [2]aionios, which is the most attractive life we could wish to live; it is the life of our design, yet it remains elusive outside the redemption that Christ achieved on our behalf. Not even the most sincere decision to live a blameless life under the law or any sincere philosophy could satisfy the heart hunger of mankind.)

2:8 Yet there are those who ignore the truth through [2]unbelief. *(The truth about their original identity as sons)* **They continue to exist as mere [1]hirelings, motivated by a monthly wage** *(rather than sonship).* **They believe in their failure and unrighteousness and are consumed by outbursts of anger and displeasure.** *(The word, [1]eithea, comes from erithos, working as a hireling for wages; often translated, self-willed or contentious. The word, [2]apeitheo, means to be not persuaded, without faith, often wrongly translated as disobedient.)*

2:9 Pressures from every side, like an [1]overcrowded room, *(or a cramped foot in an undersized shoe,)* **is the experience of the soul of everyone who does what is worthless. The fact that the Jews are Jewish does not make their experience of evil any different from that of the Greeks.** *(Symptoms of disease are the same in anyone; they are not a respecter of persons. The word, [1]stenochoria, means narrowness of room.)*

2:10 In sharp contrast to this, bliss, self-worth and total tranquillity is witnessed by everyone, both Jew and Greek, who finds expression in that which is good. We are tailor-made for good.

2:11 God does not judge people on face value.

2:12 Ruin and self-destruction are the inevitable results of sin, whether someone knows the law or not.

2:13 Righteousness is not a hearsay-thing, it is faith-inspired practical living, giving new definition to the law.

2:14 For even a pagan's natural instinct will confirm the law to be present in their conscience and though they have never even heard about Jewish laws. Thus they prove to be a law unto themselves.

2:15 The law is so much more than a mere written code; its presence in human conscience even in the absence of the written instruction is obvious, condemning or commending personal conduct.

2:16 Every hidden, conflicting thought will be disclosed in the daylight of God's scrutiny, based on the Good News of Jesus Christ that I proclaim. *(The ineffectiveness of good intentions and self discipline to produce lasting change will be exposed as worthless in contrast to the impact* *of the message of Christ's death and resurrection as representing mankind's death and new birth as our ultimate reference to our redeemed identity and innocence.)*

2:17 Your Jewish identity does not make God your exclusive property,

2:18 even though you boast in the fact that you have the [1]document-ed desire of God [2]published like an instruction manual in the law. *(The word, [1]dokimatso, comes from document, decree, approve; [2]diaphe-ro, from to carry through, to publish [Acts 13:49, the word was published throughout].)*

2:19 You promote yourself confidently as a guide for the blind, and a light bearer for those groping about in darkness.

2:20 You feel yourself so superior to the rest of the world that you promote yourself as the "kindergarten" teacher to the mindless, an instructor of infants, because you believe that in the law you have knowledge and truth all wrapped up in a nutshell.

2:21 However, the real question is not whether you are a good teach-er; how good a student are you? What's the good of teaching against stealing when you yourself steal?

2:22 You speak against adultery while you cannot get your own mind off sexual sins. It just doesn't make sense does it? You say idol-atry stinks yet you steal stuff from pagan shrines.

2:23 Your proud association with the law is ruined every time you dishonor God by dodging the doing bit.

2:24 This has been going on for hundreds of years; it is all record-ed in Scripture. No wonder the Gentiles think that your God is no better than any of their philosophies when it comes to living the life the law promotes.

2:25 The real value of circumcision is tested by your ability to keep the law. If you break the law you might as well not be circumcised.

2:26 The fact that you are circumcised does not distinguish you from the rest of the world; it does not give you super-human power to keep the commandments.

2:27 If it is not about who is circumcised or not, but rather who keeps the law or not, then in that case even uncircumcised people can judge the ones who claim to know it all and have it all! On the one hand you have those who feel naturally inclined to do what is right, yet none of them are circumcised, then you have the circum-cised who know the letter of the law but fail to keep it.

2:28 So it is not about who you appear to be on the outside that makes you a real Jew, but who you really are on the inside.

2:29 For you to know who you are in your heart is the secret of your spirit identity; this is your true circumcision, it is not the literal outward appearance that distinguishes you. After all it is God's approval and not another's opinion that matters most. People see skin-deep; God knows the heart.

3:1 Having said all this, you might ask whether there is still any advantage in being Jewish? Is there any significance in circumcision?

3:2 Everything only finds its relevance and value in the original intention of God realized by faith.

3:3 The question is, how does someone's failure to believe God affect what God believes? Can their unbelief cancel God's faith? *(What we believe about God does not define him; God's faith defines us. See the RSV translation, "What if some were unfaithful? Does their faithlessness nullify the faithfulness of God? By no means!")*

3:4 God's word is not under threat! In fact, if all of mankind fails, truth remains intact. Truth is defined in God; it is neither challenged nor vindicated by human experience. Contradiction does not intimidate or diminish God's belief. Scripture records that God stands justified in his own word; it confirms that God's promise and purpose are not compromised through mankind's failure; neither is God's reputation threatened by our behavior. *(Truth does not become true by popular vote. It is already as true as it gets because God believes it; it is from faith to faith, says Paul [Rom 1:17]; there is no gospel in it until the righteousness of God is revealed; "we can do nothing against the truth!" [See 2 Cor 13:5 and 8]. David's sin did not cancel God's promise. "But my mercy I will not take from him" and "his house shall be made sure, and his kingdom for ever before me, and his throne shall be set up forever." [2 Sam 7:15-16].)*

3:5 We could argue then that God doesn't have a right to judge us, if our unrighteousness only emphasizes his righteousness.

3:6 This would make God an unfair judge of the world.

3:7 This almost sounds like I am saying that it is not really wrong to sin, if our cheating only serves to further contrast the truth of God.

3:8 Because of my emphasis on God's grace, some people slanderously make the assumption and accuse me that my teaching would give people a license to sin. "Let us do evil that good may come!" I strongly condemn such foolish talk! *("But if our wickedness advertises the goodness of God, do we feel that God is being unfair to punish us in return? [I'm using a human tit-for-tat argument.] Not a bit of it! What sort of a person would God be then to judge the world? It is like saying that if my lying throws into sharp relief the truth of God and, so to speak, enhances his reputation, then why should he repay me by judging me a sinner? Similarly, why not do evil that good may be, by contrast all the more conspicuous and valuable? (As a matter of fact, I am reported as urging this very thing, by some slanderously and others quite seriously! But, of course, such an argument is quite properly condemned." — Rom 3:5-8 Phillips Translation.)*

3:9 It is common knowledge that sin holds the sway over both Jew and Greek alike. *(Just like disease would show the same symptoms regardless of someone's nationality.)*

3:10 Scripture records that within the context of the law, no-one succeeds to live a blameless life. *(Psalm 14:1-3, "To the choirmaster of David. The fool says in his heart, 'There is no God.' They are corrupt and they do abominable deeds, there is none that does good. The Lord looks down from heaven upon the children of men, to see if there are any that act wisely, that seek after God. They have all gone astray, they are all alike corrupt; there is none that does good, no, not one [RSV]." In Genesis 18, Abraham intercedes for Sodom and Gomorrah, "If there perhaps are 50 righteous people, will you save the city on their behalf?" He continues to negotiate with God, until he's down to, "perhaps ten?"..."there was none righteous, no not one ..." This argument is building up to the triumphant conclusion of the fact that there is indeed no distinction; the same people who fell short of the glory of God are now justified through God's work of grace in Christ. If mankind was 100% represented in Adam, then they are equally 100% represented in Christ! [Rom 3:21-24].)*

3:11 Because there seems to be no sincere craving and desire to know God there is no spiritual ¹insight. *(While a person remains casual and indifferent about God, their heart remain calloused; the word, ¹**suinemi**, means a joint-seeing.)*

3:12 Their distraction has ¹bankrupted their lives; that goes for the mass of mankind, without any exception. *(This word, ¹ נאלחו **neelachu** 'unprofitable' in Hebrew/Aramaic means to become 'putrid' and 'offensive,' like fruit that is spoiled. In Arabic, it is applied to 'milk' that becomes sour.)*

3:13 "When they open their mouth to speak they bury one another with destructive words. They snake each other with lies and corruption. *(Albert Barnes comments, "Their throat is an open sepulchre - This and all the following verses to the end of the 18th are found in the Septuagint, but not in the Hebrew text; and it is most evident that it was from this version that the apostle quoted, as the verses cannot be found in any other place with so near an approximation to the apostle's meaning and words. The verses in question, however, are not found in the Alexandrian MS. But they exist in the Vulgate, the Ethiopic, and the Arabic. As the most ancient copies of the Septuagint do not contain these verses, some contend that the apostle has quoted them from different parts of Scripture; and later transcribers of the Septuagint, finding that the 10th, 11th, and 12th, verses were quoted from the 14th Psalm, imagined that the rest were found originally there too, and so incorporated them in their copies, from the apostle's text.*

Their throat is an open sepulchre - By their malicious and wicked words they bury, as it were, the reputation of all men. The whole of this verse appears to belong to their habit of lying, defamation, slandering, etc., by which they wounded, blasted, and poisoned the reputation of others.)

3:14 With sharp tongues they ¹cut one another to pieces, cursing and cheating; their every word is inspired by the ²wearisome effort to

survive in a dog-eat- dog world. *(Taken direct from the Hebrew text in Psalm 10:7 in Hebrew, [1]tok tok* תך תך *from* ***tavek****,* תוך *to cut to pieces. In Hebrew [2]* עמל *amal and* און *aven, to exert oneself in wearisome effort.)*

3:15 Murder has become a regular ritual; without any regard for another's life.

3:16 Their path is littered with broken lives.

3:17 They have lost the art of friendship.

3:18 They have completely lost sight of God." *(3:13-18 are quotations from Psalm 10 and Psalm 14.)*

3:19 The fact that all these quotations are from Jewish writings, confirm that their law of moral conduct did not free them from the very same sins the rest of the world was trapped in. The entire human race is now confronted with the [1]righteousness of God. *(The word [1]upodikos, from* ***upo*** *under and* ***dikay****, two parties finding likeness in each other, the stem of the word* ***dikaiosunay****, righteousness. See Romans 1:17; also 3:21 and Acts 17:31, Romans 4:25.)*

3:20 The law proves all of mankind equally guilty and confirms that their most sincere duty-driven decisions and 'self-help' programs within the confines of the flesh could not give them any sense of improved confidence in their standing before God.

3:21 We are now talking a completely different language: the gospel unveils what God did right not what we did wrong! Both the law and all the prophetic writings pointed to this moment! *(This brings me back to the theme of my ministry, chapter 1:1, 2, 5, 16, 17. There is no point in telling people how condemned they are! Tell them how loved they are! God's dealing with mankind is based on the fact that their conscience continues to bear witness to their original design. Romans 7:22.)*

3:22 Jesus is what God believes about you! In him the righteousness of God is on display in such a way [1]that everyone may be equally persuaded about what God believes about them, regardless of who they are; there is [2]no distinction. *(The Preposition, [1]eis, indicates a point reached in conclusion. The Greek,* ***ou gar estin diastoley*** *means [2]there is no exception - this includes every single person, Jew and Gentile alike!)*

3:23 Mankind is in the same boat; their [1]distorted behavior is proof of a [2]lost [3]blueprint. *(The word sin, is the word [1]hamartia, from* ***ha****, negative or without and* ***meros****, portion or form, thus to be without your allotted portion or without form, pointing to a disorientated, distorted, bankrupt identity; the word* ***meros****, is the stem of* ***morphe****, as in 2 Corinthians 3:18 the word* ***metamorphe****, with form, which is the opposite of* ***hamartia*** *- without form. Sin is to live out of context with the blueprint of one's design; to behave out of tune with God's original harmony. See Deuteronomy 32:18, "You have* *forgotten the Rock that begot you and have gotten out of step with the God who danced with you!" Hebrew,* חול *khul, also means to dance, as in Jdg. 21:21. See Romans 9:33 in the Mirror! The word* ²**hustereo**, *to fall short, to be inferior,* ³**doxa**, *glory, blueprint, from* **dokeo**, *opinion or intent.)*

3:24 **While the law proved mankind's dilemma, the grace of God announces the same mankind's redemption in Jesus Christ! Their blameless innocence is a free gift! The gift-principle puts the idea of reward out of business! There is no exception - this belongs to every single person, Jew and Gentile alike!** *(v 22)* **Mankind's righteousness is now redeemed. Jesus Christ is proof of God's grace gift; he redeemed the glory of God in human life; mankind condemned in the language of religion, is now mankind justified in the language of the gospel!** *(The man Jesus Christ proved that God did not make a mistake when they made humankind in their image and likeness! Sadly the evangelical world proclaimed verse 23 completely out of context! There is no good news in verse 23, the gospel is in verse 24! All fell short because of Adam; the same 'all' are equally declared innocent because of Christ! The law reveals what happened to mankind in Adam; grace reveals what happened to the same mankind in Christ. Their is no distinction - all have sinned and fallen short of the glory of God - now they are all justified freely as a gift through the redemption [the liberating action] of Jesus Christ!)*

3:25 **Jesus exhibits God's mercy. In his blood conciliation God's faith persuades mankind of his righteousness and the fact that he has brought closure to the historic record of their sins.** *(Not by demanding a sacrifice but providing the sacrifice of himself.)* **Jesus is the unveiling of the Father's heart towards us.** *(See note to Hebrews 8:12; also 1 John 2:2.)*

3:26 **All along God** ¹**refused to let go of mankind. At this very moment God's act of** ²**righteousness is** ³**pointing them to the evidence of their innocence, with Jesus as the** ⁴**fountainhead of faith.** *(God's tolerance,* ¹**anoche**, *to echo upward; God continues to hear the echo of his likeness in us. See Rom 2:4. In both these verses [25+26] Paul uses the word,* ³**endeixis**, *where we get the word indicate from. It is also part of the stem of the word translated, righteousness,* ²**dikaiosune**. *To point out, to show, to convince with proof. Then follows,* ⁴**ek pisteos iesou; ek**, *source or origin and* **iesou** *is in the Genitive case, the owner of faith is Jesus! He is both the source and substance of faith! Hebrews 11:1, 12:2 "The Incarnation means that God Himself condescended to enter into our alienated human existence, to lay hold of it, to bind it in union with Himself; and the consummation of the Incarnation in the death and resurrection means the Son of God died for all men, and so once and for all constituted men as men upon whom God had poured out His life and love, so that men are for ever laid hold of by God and affirmed in their being as His creatures. They can no more escape from His love and sink into non-being than they can constitute themselves men for whom Christ has not died. How can God go back upon the death of His dear Son?*

How can God undo the Incarnation and go back upon Himself? How can God who is Love go back upon the pouring out of His love once and for all and so cease to be Himself? That is the decisive, final thing about the whole Incarnation including the death of Christ, that it affects all men, indeed the whole of creation, for the whole of creation is now put on a new basis with God, the basis of a Love that does not withhold itself but only overflows in our unending Love.

That is why creation still continues in being, and that is why man still exists, for God has not given him up, but on the contrary poured out His love upon him unreservedly once and for ever, decidedly and finally affirming man as His child, eternally confirming the creation as His own handiwork. God does not say Yes, and No, for all He has done is Yes and Amen in Christ. That applies to every man, whether he will or no. He owes his very being to Christ and belongs to Christ, and in that he belongs to Christ he has his being only from Him and in relation to Him." Thomas F. Torrance courtesy Baxter Kruger's study notes.)

3:27 The law of faith cancels the law of works; which means there is suddenly nothing left for anyone to boast in. No one is superior to another. *(Bragging only makes sense if there is someone to compete with or impress. "While we compete with one another and compare ourselves with one another we are without understanding. [2 Corinthians 10:12]. "Through the righteousness of God we have received a faith of equal standing."*

[See 2 Peter 1:1 RSV] The OS (operating system) of the law of works is will-power; the OS of the law of faith is love. Galatians 5:6 Love sets faith in motion. The law presented one with choices; grace awakens belief! Willpower exhausts, love ignites! If choices could save us we would be our own Saviors! Willpower is the language of the law, love is the language of grace and it ignites faith that leads to romance; falling in love beats "making a decision to believe in love" by far! See Rom 7:19 Willpower has failed me; this is how embarrassing it is, the most diligent decision that I make to do good, disappoints.)

3:28 This leaves us with only one logical conclusion, mankind is justified by God's faith and not by their ability to keep the law.

3:29 Which means that God is not the private property of the Jews but belongs equally to all the nations. *(While the law excludes the non-Jewish nations, faith includes us all on level terms.)*

3:30 There is only one God, he deals with everyone, circumcised or uncircumcised exclusively on the basis of faith.

3:31 No, faith does not re-write the rules; instead it confirms that the original life-quality meant for mankind as mirrored and documented in the 10 commandments, is now realized in the Gospel. *(Jesus brought closure to the old in his death and introduced the new dimension in his resurrection.)*

In the following chapters, Paul further embroiders his powerful logic and revelation of mankind's redemption. *[As highlighted in Romans 1:16,17 & 2:24-29 and here in chapter 3, especially verses 20-31]*

He now continues in Chapter 4, reminding his audience of their ancestor Abraham.

Faith-righteousness was not Abram's idea or invention. He was simply overwhelmed by his Maker's belief and favor, in his God-encounters! See Genesis 12-17 to begin with. Only then *[in chapter 17]*, he became Abra<u>ha</u>m; when God added the *hey* of their own name יהוה Jaweh in his name. The letter ה *hey*, in Ancient Hebrew is, ⛫ the man with raised hands pictures a sigh of wonder, "behold," as when looking at a great sight; thus, meaning, "breath" or "sigh," as one does when seeing something wonderful and pointing it out. The ה *[hey]* is also the number 5, which is the number for grace.

No, it was not Abram's faith that rewarded him with righteousness! Faith is not something we do; it is what happens to us when we encounter the Agape of God! There is only ONE faith! Ephesians 4:5. Jesus is both the Source and sustenance of this faith! Hebrews 12:2. Also Romans 1:17 & 2:21,22.

In my book, Divine Embrace, I have a chapter on Incarnate Faith which addresses the statement of Jesus, "Let it be to you according to <u>your faith</u>."

Also here, https://www.mirrorword.net/mirror-study-bible-faq

4:1 If we look at our father Abraham as an example and scrutinize his life, would you say that he discovered any reason for placing confidence in the flesh through personal contribution?

4:2 If he felt that his friendship with God was a reward for good behavior, then surely he would have reason to recommend the recipe; yet it is plain to see that it was all God's initiative from start to finish.

4:3 Scripture is clear, Abraham reflected God's belief in him; this is the basis of the [1]rediscovery of [2]righteousness. (*[1]One must remember that in Adam & Eve's communion with Elohim, something was lost which would be redeemed - there would be a "return" to the consciousness of this union. [2]This most significant, relational term, righteousness, points to a shared likeness; this includes one's authentic identity and innocence. The word [2]dikaiosune, righteousness is from the stem dike, two parties finding likeness in each other. Also, note that the name of the Greek goddess of Justice is Dike [pronounced, Dikey]; she is always pictured holding a scale of balances in her hand.*)

4:4 There is a large difference between a reward and a gift: if you have earned something through hard work, then what you receive in return is your due and certainly not a gift.

4:5 Righteousness as God's free gift, takes the idea of reward out of the equation - faith and not our toil celebrates the innocence of the ungodly!

4:6 David confirms this principle when he speaks of the blessedness of the one who discovers God's approval without any reference to something specific that they had done to qualify themselves.

4:7 Oh what [1]happy progress one makes with the weight of sin and guilt removed and one's slate wiped clean. (*The Greek, μακάριος makarios, means extremely blessed/happy. The Aramaic/Hebrew word [1]ashar, אשׁר blessed, means to advance, to make progress.*)

4:8 "How blessed is the one who receives a [1]receipt instead of an invoice for their sins." (*[1]logitzomai, to make a calculation to which there can only be one logical conclusion, to take an inventory. LXX-Psalm 31:1, 2; Masoretic Hebrew Text -Psalm 32:1, 2*)

4:9 Now, is the blessedness that we are talking about restricted exclusively to the circumcised, or are those who have never even heard about the "cut" equally included? Remember we are looking at Abraham *[in whom all nations are blessed]*, as our example of a righteousness that is purely based upon the principle of a faith sourced in God's persuasion. (*Note, ἡ πίστις, he pistis, the faith. There is only one valid source of faith, not what we believe about God or about ourselves, but what God believes about us. Romans 1:17; 2:22*)

4:10 So, the question is, was he reckoned righteous before or after he was circumcised? It is clear that Abraham's faith-encounters *[as recorded in Genesis 12 through 15],* **happened long before circumcision was mentioned!** *(The symbolic circumcision covenant was only introduced years later in Genesis 17, when he was already 99 years old. [Isaac's birth is only recorded in Genesis 21.]*

See my **notes on circumcision** *at the end of this chapter.)*

4:11 Thus, Abraham received circumcision as an external, symbolic [1]seal to remind him of what God has already [2]declared many years ago, when he was first introduced to the concept of "the [3]righteousness of God". Since Abraham's supernatural fatherhood is celebrated in circumcision, it infers that he is both the father of Jew and Gentile alike - God already engaged him in covenant as an uncircumcised Gentile - he thus represents them in all that was predicted concerning the blessing of every nation in the Seed of faith!

([1] A [1]seal of the righteousness of the faith - **sphragida tēs dikaiosunēs tēs pisteōs***. The [1]seal of circumcision, was not meant to be a distraction but rather a prophetic confirmation to the only valid basis to "the righteousness [of God]" by the principle of the faith [of God]. Just like a receipt is only a reference to, and not the actual transaction. Note, the faith and the righteousness. See 2 Corinthians 13:5. Also here in Romans 4:25.*

[2] Circumcision did not introduce an adjusted or new covenant - it was simply added as a symbolic seal in [2]confirmation to God's resolve, as recorded in Genesis 12:2,3 and Genesis 15:5. In the meantime, Abraham's moments of unbelief, delays and detours did not distract from God's determined destiny for the prophetic Messianic Seed. **Galatians 3:16** *It is on record that the promise [of the blessing of righteousness by God's faith] was made to Abraham and to his Seed, singular, [thus excluding his effort to produce Ishmael.] Isaac, the child of promise, and not of the flesh, mirrors the Messiah. [Genesis 3:15])*

4:12 At the same time he also represents all Jews as their father; especially those, for whom circumcision is not merely a skin deep religious ritual, but who engages the same principle of the faith that ignited Abraham's belief.

4:13 [1]Righteousness by faith and not righteousness by law prompted the promise when God announced to Abraham that he would father those who would inherit the world. It is again a matter of embracing a gift rather than receiving a reward for keeping the law.

"Look away [from the law of works] unto Jesus; he is the Author and finisher of faith." [Hebrews 12:2]. It is God's faith to begin with; it is **from faith to faith***, and not our good or bad behavior; we are not defined by our performance or circumstances. The Greek word translated "from" is the Preposition,* **ek***, which always denotes source or origin. The language*

of the old written code was, "Do in order to become. The language of the new is, "Be, because of what was done." Instead of do, do, do, it's done, done, done. Paul refers here to **Habakkuk 2:4, "The just shall live by his [God's] faith."** *Habakkuk sees a complete new basis to mankind's standing before God. Instead of reading the curse when disaster strikes, he realizes that the Promise out-dates performance as the basis to mankind's acquittal. The curse is taken out of the equation. Galatians 3:13.*

4:14 **Faith would be emptied of its substance and the principle of promise would be meaningless if the law of personal performance was still in play, to qualify the heirs.** *(Faith is not in competition with the law. The life quality that faith reveals is consistent with mankind's original design and mirrors the very life that the law promotes.)*

4:15 **The law system is bound to bring about disappointment, regret and anger; if there is no law there is nothing to break; no contract, no breach.**

4:16 **Therefore since faith sponsors the gift of grace, the promise is equally secured for all the children. The law has no exclusive claim on anyone** *[the reward system cannot match the gift principle].* **Faith is our source, and this makes Abraham our father.**

4:17 **When God changed Abram's name to Abraham, he made a public statement that he would be the father of all nations.** *[Genesis 17]* **Here we see Abraham faced with God's faith; the kind of faith that resurrects the dead and calls things which are not** *[yet visible in planet earth's time-zone],* **as though they were.** *(See my extended notes at the end of this chapter.)*

4:18 **Faith gave substance to hope when everything seemed hopeless; the words, "so shall your seed be" conceived in him the faith of fatherhood.** *(Abraham's case here pictures the hopelessness of fallen mankind, having lost their identity, and faced with the impossibility to redeem themselves.)*

4:19 **Abraham's faith would have been nullified if he were to take his own age and the deadness of Sarah's womb into account. His hundred year old body and Sarah's barren womb did not distract him in the least. He finally knew that no contribution from their side could possibly assist God in fulfilling the promise.**

4:20 **While he had every reason to doubt, he did not hesitate for a moment but instead, empowered by faith's persuasion, he continued to communicate God's opinion.** *(His name was his confession: in the Hebrew language, "Abraham"* אברהם *was not a mere familiar sounding name, but a meaningful sentence, a confession of faith's authority, against the odds. He did not become embarrassed about his name; he did not change his name to "Abe" for short when there seemed to be no change in his circumstances. Every time he introduced himself or someone called him by his name, it was a* *bold declaration and repetition of God's promise, calling things that were not as though they were. I would imagine that Sarah spoke his name the most. In fact, every time they addressed one another they spoke the promise, "Mother of nations, kings of peoples shall come from you." [Genesis 17:5, 16]. Abraham, "the father of the multitudes.")*

4:21 Abraham's confidence was his [1]dress-code; he knew beyond doubt that the power of God to perform was equal to his promise. *([1]plerophoreo, from plero to be completely covered in every part, + phoreo, to wear garments or armor; traditionally translated to be completely persuaded. His faith was his visible identity and armor; he wore his persuasion like he would his daily garments.)*

4:22 The persuasion of God rubbed off on Abraham and became his personal conviction. This is the [1]basis of righteousness. *("Righteousness was [1]reckoned to him," this means that God's faith pointed Abraham to an invisible future where mankind's innocence and identity would be redeemed again. Greek, [1]logitsomai, logical conclusion.)*

4:23 Here is the Good News: the recorded words, "It was reckoned to him" were not written for his sake alone.

4:24 Scripture was written with us in mind. We are audience to the same faith in the face of death. The same [1]conclusion is now equally relevant in our realizing the significance of Jesus' resurrection from the dead. *(By raising Jesus from the dead God proclaims his belief in our redeemed innocence. Isaac's birth from Sarah's barren womb prophetically declared the resurrection of Jesus from the tomb. Abraham's best efforts could not produce Isaac. Sarah's dead womb is a picture of the impossibility of the flesh to produce a child. This underlines mankind's inability to redeem themselves under the performance-based law of willpower.*

Jesus said, "Abraham saw my day." Mankind's most extreme self-sacrifice offered in an attempt to win the favorable attention of their deity could never match the sacrifice of God's Lamb to win the attention of mankind. When Isaac questioned his father about the sacrifice, then Abraham announced, "Jahweh jireh." יהוה יראה Jahweh sees. And he lifted up his eyes and behold **behind him** *was a ram caught in the thorn bush by its horns. Note, "Behind him." Faith sees the future in past tense-mode.*

The resurrection is the ultimate proof and trophy of righteousness by God's faith. [See Rom 6:11] [1]logitsomai - logical conclusion. "Consider [logitsomai] yourself dead indeed," compared with 4:19, "Abraham considered his own body dead." We can only study Scripture in the context of Christ as representing the human race; God had us in mind all along [John 5:39].)

4:25 While our [1]sins [2]resulted in his death; our righteousness and redeemed innocence is [2]celebrated in his resurrection!

([1] *The word* [1]***parapiptō*** *has two components,* ***para***, *closest possible proximity of union, and* ***piptō***, *to descend from a higher place to a lower; to fall; to be thrust down; from* ***petomai***, *to fly. Thus to stop flying. Losing altitude. This speaks of mankind's short falling, or their fallen mindset. Romans 3:23,24; Also, Col 3:1-3. See* ***Philippians 3:10***, *Oh to comprehend the dynamic of his resurrection. His resurrection is evidence of our righteousness.*

[2] *It is most wonderful to discover that his resurrection does not include us only once we believe! If something is not true to begin with, our belief will not make it true!*

Paul uses the word, ***dia*** *twice in this verse! Unfortunately most translations in most languages only translate the 1st* ***dia*** *correctly!*

He was handed over <u>BECAUSE of</u> [***dia***] *our sins - why was he raised?*

NOT so that some small portion of the "elite christian group" may stand a dim chance to be justified!!!

NO! Hallelujah! The same word, ***dia*** *is used again!*

He was raised <u>BECAUSE of</u> [***dia***] *our righteousness!*

Here is the equation:

His cross = our sins,

His resurrection = our innocence.

His resurrection is the official receipt to our acquittal. This is one of the most important statements in the entire Bible. His death brought closure to our short falling; his resurrection is proof of our redeemed righteousness.

His resurrection reveals our righteousness. If mankind was still guilty after Jesus died, his resurrection would be irrelevant. This explains Acts 10:28 and 2 Corinthians 5:14 and 16.

See Young's Literal Translation, Romans 4:25 "who was delivered up because of our offences, and was raised up because of our being declared righteous."

In Acts 17:31, Paul explains to the Greek philosophers that according to the Jewish prophetic word, "God had fixed a day on which he would judge the world in righteousness by a man whom he has appointed, and of this he has given proof to all mankind by raising him from the dead." God's declaration of your redeemed innocence is his most urgent invitation to you[manity] to encounter intimate oneness.

See also 1 Peter 1:10-12 "This salvation which you now know as your own, is the theme of the prophetic thought; this is what captured the Prophets' attention for generations and became the object of their most diligent inquiry and scrutiny. They knew all along that mankind's salvation was a grace revelation, sustained in their prophetic utterance. [Salvation would never be by personal achievement or a reward to willpower-driven initiative. The law of works would never replace grace.]

1 Pet 1:11 In all of their conversation there was a constant quest to determine who the Messiah would be, and exactly when this will happen. They knew with certainty that it was the spirit of Christ within them pointing prophetically and giving testimony to the sufferings of the Christ and the subsequent glory. [Whatever glory was lost in Adam, would be redeemed again in Jesus Christ.]

1 Pet 1:12 It was revealed to them that this glorious grace message that they were communicating pointed to a specific day and person beyond their own horizon and generation; they saw you in their prophetic view. This heavenly announcement had you in mind all along. They proclaimed glad tidings to you in advance, in the Holy Spirit, commissioned from heaven; the celestial messengers themselves longed to gaze deeply into its complete fulfillment.")

Notes on Circumcision

Notes on Circumcision

Notes on Circumcision

In symbolic-language, circumcision communicates that the son of man is the son of God, and not the fruit of his natural father's seed. There is only ONE Father of the human race. Malachi 2:10 & Ephesians 3:15.

So, what makes childless, "pagan" Abram, such a key candidate to be the carrier of the Seed of Promise?

<u>Consider the meaning of his grandfather and father's names</u>:

*Abram's grandfather is **Nahor** נחור, meaning nose, inhaling the breath of life; in Ancient Hebrew [also reading from right to left] , ꓤ ꭐ ꓘ a picture of a seed sprout, representing the idea of continuing into a new generation; ꭐ for the letter ח ch, like in the sound, ch in the word, Bach - it is a picture of a tent wall, to protect the occupants from the elements outside; the head of a person, ꓤ can also represent the mind; thus, to see an offspring, protected in the tent walls of a person's mind. As Abraham's grandfather, Nahor's name carries the prophetic word in-spite of the seeming "delay" in both of the births of his son **Terah** תרח [meaning delay!], as well as his grandson Abram!*

***Abram** אברם; the first two letters Aleph and Bet, **Ab** אב means father, and **ram**, רם in Hebrew is exalted; above, as in the heavenly dimension. In Ancient Hebrew, ꭐꓳ the head of a young bull - strength and ꭐ tent, house; strength of the house; thus, meaning father or head of the house. Then follows the word, רם ram, The letter r, is the head of a person, ꓤ which also represents the mind, and the letter m, ꭠ as a picture of water or the sea representing mass, also the heavenly dimension*

*Note that most of Abram's ancestors were already fathers at the ages of 29 or 35; yet his own father, **Terah** תרח [meaning, **delay!**] was 70 years old before he had **Abram**; אברם his name suggests that Terah acknowledged that he could not claim parenthood of this son, he was 'fathered from above'! [Genesis 11:12-26]*

Now imagine how nervous Abram was, when he was 75 [In Haran] and still without a child.

<u>Abram's early life</u>

Abram's first 70 years are rooted in Babylonian culture, most of which represents man's failed attempts to reach beyond their earthbound horizon; as in the tower of Babel, which then spiralled out into a confusion of languages, philosophies and religions. Their quest continued to be expressed in the many **Zigurrats**, which were a type of rectangular, very high temple tower or tiered mound erected by the Sumerians, Akkadians, and Babylonians in Mesopotamia. *[Like the Great Ziggurat of Ur, the capital of the ancient Chaldean Empire where Abram stems from.]*

39

The Chaldeans were the learned class; they were farmers, traders, priests, magicians and astronomers.

*The Greek word Χαλδαῖος **Chaldaios**, referring to a native of the region of the lower Euphrates bordering on the Persian Gulf. In Hebrew, **kaśdîy** - בַּשְׂדִי meaning, **clod breakers** - from the root, keśed כֶּשֶׂד Chesed, "increase".*

The extraordinary fertility of the Chaldaean soil has been noticed by various writers. It is said to be the only country in the world where wheat grows wild.

*The name Babel is etymologised by associations with the Hebrew verb **balal**, "to confuse or confound". The word **Bab-ilu** "Gate of God" in Akkadian language, **bab**, gate + **ilu**, god; or its Sumerian name, **E-temen-an-ki** means, house of the foundation of heaven on earth.*

An amazing prophetic mirror unfolds 1500 years later! Israel is taken captive into Babylon for 70 years! They have metaphorically returned to the "dormant womb" of Abram's 70 years in Babylon before Jaweh broke the silence! *[Representing the failure of the entire religious Jewish-Levitical and institutionalized Christian-order! Which would sadly be the repeat-cycle of their own blindfolds until the ends of the earth returns to the Lord in their realizing and re-discovering their redeemed sonship. Ps 22:27; Psalm 110:4; Hebrews 6:20 & chapter 7]*

Jeremiah 29:10 For thus says the LORD: After seventy years are completed at Babylon, I will visit you and perform My good word toward you, and cause you to return to this place. *[The Promised land - symbolically pointing to the entire human person, both individually, as well as globally]*

Jeremiah 29:11 For I know the thoughts that I think toward you, says the LORD, thoughts of peace and not of evil, to give you a future and a hope.

Meanwhile, Abram is stuck in a conversation that has, instead of leading him through "the Gate of God", entangled him in a cul-de-sac, pagan religion. His accumulated wealth wouldn't buy him and Sarai a child! Yet, he held on to a fragile thread of hope, since his father Terah only conceived him when he was 70 years old.

Abram's God-encounters

It was at this time, that he encounters God, who conceives in him *a new conversation* - the seed theme of the promise to Eve, is revived.

Genesis 3:15 Your seed shall crush the head of the serpent! [Representing the mindset of the "I am not-Tree"; I have to strive to be.]

God, very intentionally and at various intervals, continues to meet with landless, and childless Abram, for the next 30 years, from Ur in ancient Macedonia to Haran; then, at various locations, in Shechem, Mamre, Bethel, Canaan and Valley of Shaveh *(that is, the King's Valley)*.

In Genesis 15:5, God engages Abraham with a larger dimension than his present circumstantial horizon - "Lift up your eyes! - Realize how impossible it is to count the stars! So shall your seed be!

At that point, faith happened! The very next verse reads, Genesis 15:6 "Abraham believed what God believed about him and that concluded his righteousness."

Time and again God confirms to him, that in his Seed, all the families of the earth shall be blessed! See Genesis 12:1-3; Genesis 13-17 & Acts 7:2-5. Genesis 15:7, "I am the LORD, who led you out of Ur in Babylonia..."

A glimpse of Abram's wealth, fortitude and strategic skills. None of which would succeed in fulfilling the promise of his own offspring.

> Genesis 14 describes the battle of nine kings, but then, while living in Mamre, Abram the Hebrew, hears that his brother's son Lot's is taken captive. *[This is the 1st time the word Hebrew is used* עבר *Heyber is connected with crossing over and the beyond. Abram by now, has this reputation of traveling beyond boundaries and difficulties.]*
>
> He then mustered 318 of his servants, skilled in warfare - all of them born in his household - and pursued the captors for a hundred and twenty miles, all the way to Dan. There, he and his men split into small groups and attacked by night. They chased them as far as Hobah, and defeated them just north of Damascus. Thus they recovered all the loot, along with nephew Lot and his possessions, including the women and the people. Genesis 14:14-16

Melchizedek and the Covenant meal

And now on his victorious return, he encounters *a tenth king,* Melchizedek, King of Righteousness, the King of Salem *[the king of peace]*, who did not partake in the Canaanite warfare but, in his King/Priestly capacity, blesses Abram and shares with him the covenant meal of bread and wine. *(See my notes on* **Understanding the significance of meals in Covenant context** *at the end of Luke 11.)*

Furthermore, the king of Sodom desires to reward Abram with the spoils of war - but, he refuses to take even a shoestring, "so that you may not say, I have made Abram rich!" Instead, he gives a tenth of the spoils to the tenth King, Mechizedek!

> *Genesis 15:1 in the Septuagint LXX reads,* **Immediately after Abram meets Mechizedek, Jahweh speaks to him and addresses his fears** *[no land; no child]* **"Fear not! Beyond all comparison** *[υπερασπιζω from*

ὑπεράνω huperanō; uper + ano - over and above], I am your priceless reward; exceedingly surpassing any possible reward you could wish for, as achieved in by your own efforts!

See **Hebrews 7:3 There exists no record that can link Melchizedek to a natural father or mother; no birth certificate neither any account of his death, nor is there any record of his age.**

He resembles exactly the Son of God: his priesthood abides without beginning or end. *[This was at a time where detailed records were kept of every genealogy. This encounter greatly boosts Abram's faith!]*

Hebrews 7:10 When Melchizedek and Abraham met, Levi was already present in the loins of his father. *[By the time Levi was born, Melchizedek was still alive; since he has no beginning of time nor end of life,* **in him time and eternity meet.** *]*

In **Psalm 110:4** *[***109** *in LXX] David announces the Messianic priesthood after the order of Melchizedek; which will eclipse the Levitical order [of natural birth].*

Bread and wine points to the ultimate covenant.

The cutting of covenants involved the shedding of blood, which was a familiar practice between two parties in those times. *In Hebrew,* כרת ברית *karat berit literally means to cut a covenant. [Even our modern day handshake still reminds of the symbolic mingling of blood between two parties]*

In Ancient Hebrew, also reading from right to left, †⌐ᕳ◻ †ᕳᴲ *the letter* ᴲ*, or* כ *k-sound, pictures a open palm presenting a free-will offering; then the "r",* ᕳ *the head or mind; followed by the letter "t", Tau* † *the cross! Karat translates to "cut". Then the word, covenant* ברית *berit, or in Ancient Hebrew,* †⌐ᕳ◻ *the letter "B" is the house; then the persons head* ᕳ *- the head of the house; then the "i"* י *Jod,* ⌐ *is an outstretched arm reaching into our lostness [our "out of homeness"] in order to rescue us. Then the Tau* † *which is the last letter of the Hebrew alphabet - the fulfilment of the conversation. This is a powerful picture of the Cross of Christ - the covenant of salvation. Philippians 2:8-11.*

In Genesis 15:13-17, God instructs him to cut the animals in half; with the two halves representing and mirroring the two parties; both parties would typically walk between these pieces and declare their mutual covenant commitment, based on various conditions. Yet, in Abram's case, he fell into a deep sleep. *[This reminds of Adam - Eve was not an after-thought! Adam was put into a deep sleep; then God took her out of the word that was already made flesh! Mankind redeemed, the Bride, began the same way! Co-quickened, co-raised we are!]*

And, while Abram was fast asleep, Jaweh spoke to him about future generations of his seed. Then, God moved between the mirror-pieces in a smoking fire pot and a flaming torch. *[The prophetic pointer to God's act of redemption in the Messiah. [Also the trinity of 3 animals - three years old - representing the 3 years of Jesus ministry of Salvation.]*

Jesus crucified between two criminals is the ultimate **Mirror Covenant.**

1 Corinthians 11:23-25, The night in which the Lord Jesus was betrayed, he took bread and gave thanks; breaking the bread into portions, he said, "Realize your association with my death, every time you eat, remember my body that was broken for you." He did exactly the same with the cup after supper and said, "This cup holds the wine of the New Covenant in my blood; you celebrate me every time you drink with this understanding." *(From now on our meals are meaningful. We celebrate the fact that the incarnation reveals our redemption; the promise became a person.*

Romans 4:2... it is plain to see that it was all God's initiative from start to finish. Romans 4:3 Scripture is clear, Abraham reflected God's belief in him; this is the basis of the rediscovery of righteousness.

Also, **Hebrews 6:13 Since God had no one greater by whom to swear, he swore by himself. He could give Abraham no greater guarantee but the integrity of his own Being; this makes the promise as sure as God is.**

Abram awakens to an unconditional covenant. *[James, the younger brother of Jesus, calls it the perfect law of liberty, ἐλεύθερος **eleutheros**, unrestrained; exempt from obligation or liability!]*

Circumcision follows a game-changer Name Change!

Finally, at the age of 99 *[Genesis 17]*, when everything still seems rather hopeless, God introduces Abram to **Abraham**! He adds the letter 'ה *he'*, the breath of life, of יהוה Jahweh's own name into Abram's name and he becomes, *Abra<u>ha</u>m* אברהם the father of the multitudes of nations.

And, in Ancient Hebrew, ᴍ𐤇𐤀𐤌ᶲ *The letter* ה *h, in Ancient Hebrew is* 𐤀 *man with the raised hands pictures a sigh of wonder."behold," as when looking at a great sight; thus, meaning, "breath" or "sigh," as one does when seeing something wonderful and pointing it out. The* ה *[he] is also the number 5, which is the number for grace!*

There is no Hebrew word, -raham but, in Arabic the word means drizzling and lasting rain. The innumerable drops of water in the rain are like the stars mentioned in **Genesis 15:5** "Look toward heaven, and number the stars, if you are able to number them - so shall your seed be!" Now, imagine those innumerable stars raining down upon the earth and each one becomes a grain of sand!

> **Genesis 22:17** "I will indeed bless you, and I will multiply your Seed as the stars of heaven and as the sand which is on the seashore."

In **Genesis 17:4-5** *God announces him as the father of the masses of nations* אב המון גוים, *ab hamon goyim; The word* המון, *hamon, does not express simply a large number, but the rain-like noise that emerges from a unified, seething throng of people!*

Abraham's identity, his name, was the echo of God's faith and his bold confession in the absence of Isaac.

> *This significant name change reminds of* **Matthew 16:17** *Blessed are you, Simon, son of Jonah! [Bar Jonah, his surname identity] Flesh and blood did not reveal this to you, but My Father! I say, you are Rock, a chip [**petros**] of the old Block [**petra**]! And upon this revelation, that the son of man is the son of God, I will build my **ekklesia** and the gates of **Hades** will not prevail against it.*

> *The **ekklesia** from **ek**, source/origin and **kaleo**, to surname; original identity. **Hades**, from **ha**, negative particle, and **eido** to see. In a walled city, the gates are the most strategic point - if the gates are disengaged, the city is taken! Thus, the blindfold mode of mankind's forgotten identity, will not prevail against you!*

Also See **Deuteronomy 32:4**, "Ascribe greatness to our God, the Rock! His work is perfect and all his ways are just! A God of faithfulness, righteous and upright is he."

Deuteronomy 32:18, "But you were unmindful of the Rock that begot you, and forgot the God who gave you birth."

Also **Isaiah 51:1,2** Look to the Rock from which you were hewn, the quarry from which you were dug!

Look to Abraham your father and to Sarah who bore you; for when he was but one I called him, and I blessed him and made him many.

Now God introduces Abraham to the covenant of circumcision.

We have said that circumcision symbolically communicates that **the son of man is the son of God**, and not the fruit of his natural father's seed! There is only ONE Father of the human race. Malachi 2:10 & Ephesians 3:15; Ephesians 4:6.

Notes on Circumcision

While this circumcision-mirror-covenant does not involve an animal or bird *[as in Genesis 15]*; it will engage Abram in a most personal way; perhaps, the most sensitive and very significant member of the male human body, the foreskin of the penis! Here is the profound connection, not only does this member feature prominently in sexual intimacy, but entire future generations are represented in it.

In this circumcision-cut, God is saying to Abraham that the very member of his body which failed to produce the promised Seed, will now remind him of the covenant of promise. That, in the prophetic Seed of the Promise, all the nations of the earth will be blessed with their redeemed, restored identity and innocence. *[Righteousness]* The authentic life of their design will be rebooted in resurrected hope!

In **Genesis 17:10,11**, we have the first mention of the words connected with circumcision. God again repeats the fact that the fruit of his seed, *[τοῦ σπέρματός σου]* **sperma** *in Greek, and* זרע **zera**, *in Hebrew; will be exceedingly multiplied..." [Which reminds of John 12:24, The single grain of wheat will not abide alone - it will bear much fruit]*

> [1] *The term, translated* [1]**circumcision** *περιτέμνω* **peritemno**, *is from* **peri**, *around, and τομώτερος* **tomōteros** *a derivative of τέμνω* **temno** *to cut with precision; and in Hebrew* לומ **mul**, *to cut off.*

> [2] *Then the term, ἀκροβυστία* [2]**akrobustia** *from ἄκρον* **akron** *the tip, and πόσθη* **posthē** *- the penis. In the Tanach [Jewish Bible] the Hebrew word for* [2]*foreskin is,* עורלה *'orlá.*

This significant covenant-cut is intended to symbolically remind every circumcised male, that the son of man is the son of God! Both our eternal Genesis, as well as our eternal Destiny are endorsed. The Father of creation, in whom we live and move and have our being, is metaphorically communicated in this covenant of remembrance.

Everyday, the circumcised penis would represent this profound, and figurative token; whether the man reliefs his bladder or enjoys intimacy - the reminder is evident!

> **"I bless the Lord for** [1]**bringing understanding to me. Also in the nights, when my** [2]**kidneys prompt me** *[to get up and go for a "leak"],* **they instruct me." Psalm 16:7.** *(The word, συνετίσαντά, Aorist Participle of* [1]*συνετιζω to bring to an awareness. The word, νεφροι* [2]**nephroi** *refers to kidneys; also, one's inner promptings/thoughts.)*

<u>So shall your Seed be...</u>

> *See* **Galatians 3:16** **It is on record that the promise** *[of the blessing of righteousness by God's faith]* **was made to Abraham and to his Seed, singular,** *[thus excluding his effort to produce Ishmael.]* **Isaac, the child of promise, and not of the flesh, mirrors the Messiah.**

Romans 4:18 Faith gave substance to hope when everything seemed hopeless; the words, "so shall your seed be" conceived in Abraham the faith of fatherhood. *(Abraham's case here pictures the hopelessness of fallen mankind, having lost their identity, and faced with the impossibility to redeem themselves.)*

Romans 4:19 Abraham's faith would have been nullified if he were to take his own age and the deadness of Sarah's womb into account. His hundred year old body and Sarah's barren womb did not distract him in the least. He finally knew that no contribution from their side could possibly assist God in fulfilling his promise.

Romans 4:20 While he had every reason to doubt the promise, he did not hesitate for a moment but instead, empowered by faith confidence, he continued to communicate God's opinion. *(His name was his confession: in the Hebrew language, "Abraham" אברהם was not a mere familiar sounding name, but a meaningful sentence, a confession of faith's authority, against the odds. He was not embarrassed about his name; he did not change his name to "Abe" for short, when there seemed to be no change in his circumstances. Every time he introduced himself, or someone called him by his name, it was a bold declaration and repetition of God's promise, calling things that were not as though they were. I would imagine that Sarah spoke his name the most. In fact, every time they addressed one another they spoke the promise, "Mother of nations, kings of peoples shall come from you." [Gen 17:5, 16]. Abraham, "the father of the multitudes.")*

The Seed of David

Jesus' grandfather, from his mother's side, was Eli, עלי *- meaning, elevation; to raise above; ascension. In Luke 3:23, Luke records the genealogy of Jesus by beginning with Mary's father, Eli. He confirms the prophetic word pointing to the virgin birth, "Ask a sign of the LORD your God; let it be deep as Sheol or high as heaven. But you would not, therefore the Lord himself will give you a sign. Behold, a virgin shall conceive and bear a Son, and shall call his name Immanuel." Isaiah 7:11-14.*

See **Luke 1:27 Gabriel was to visit Mary, a [1]young, virgin girl, engaged to marry Joseph, a descendant of David.** *(The word [1]parthenos, literally, "from Athens" - an epithet meaning "Virgin", applied by the Greeks to several goddesses, especially Athena. Always associated with a virgin girl - as in LXX Isa 7:14. [The LXX was the Jewish Scriptures of the time. The Septuagint, from the Latin: septuāgintā literally "seventy"; often abbreviated as 70 in Roman numerals, i.e., LXX; sometimes called the Greek Old Testament. It is the earliest extant Koine Greek translation of the Hebrew Scriptures. [It was at the request of Ptolemy II Philadelphus (285–247 BCE) by 70 Jewish scholars or, according to later tradition,*

72, with six scholars from each of the Twelve Tribes of Israel.] The discovery of the Qumran scrolls reveal that the LXX represents much older manuscripts than our OT, which used the 1000 years later Masoretic text.] **In the Masoretic text the word virgin was changed to, an unmarried girl.)**

This also endorses the earliest prophetic reference to the Messiah's triumph over the serpent mindset - "The seed of the woman shall crush the serpent's head!" Genesis 3:15.

Matthew writes the genealogy of Joseph, descended from David via Solomon, while Luke connects Jesus with David via Nathan! See, 2 Sam 5:14, David's children, born in Jerusalem: Shammua, Shobab, Nathan, Solomon.

Also **Romans 1:3 The Son of God has his natural lineage from the seed of David.**

The prophet **Micah,** מיכה *[meaning, who is like God],* wrote, **"And you, Bethlehem, belonging to the house of Ephrathah; you are the least among the thousands of Judah; yet, my ruler in Israel will emerge out of you; this One's origin is from the beginning, whose lineage can be traced to the Ancient of Days." Micah 5:2.**

Jesus quotes a very prominent Messianic Psalm in, **Luke 20:42-44 David himself says, Jahweh said to my Lord, sit at my right hand, until I have subdued your enemies under your feet.** *[Ps 109:1 LXX - Ps 110 MS]* **So, if David calls him my Lord, how can he be his son?**

Jesus, knowing that prophetic scripture is all about him [Luke 24:27], now engages this Psalm of David; every Jew and especially their Scribes would recognize it as a most significant Messianic prophecy. Imagine the courage flooding Jesus' spirit as he mirrored this crucial moment in Scripture. By quoting the opening verse of a Psalm; every Scribe immediately knows that the entire Psalm is intended. See my commentary on Psalm 109 [Ps 110] at the end of Luke 20.

No wonder then that he says in **Matthew 23:9 You must not call** *[μὴ καλέσητε]* **anyone here on earth Father, because you have only the one Father in heaven.**

1 Cor 8:6 "There is only one God, the Father, who is the Creator of all things and for whom we live; and there is only one Lord, Jesus Christ, through whom all things were created and through whom we live."

Before Abraham was, I am.

John 1:1 To go back to the very [1]beginning, is to find the [2]Word already [3]present there; [4]face to face with God. The one mirrors the other. The Word is [3]I am; God's [2]eloquence echoes and [4]concludes in him. The Word equals God.

*In the beginning, [1]***arche,*** *to be first in order, time, place or rank.*

The Word, [2]logos, [intelligence as an interconnected network of things known; the sum total of logic] was "with" God; here and again in verse 2, John uses the Greek Preposition [4]pros, towards; face-to-face.

Three times in this sentence John uses the Active Indicative Imperfect form of the verb [3]eimi, namely **aen** *[ἦν] to continue to be, [in the beginning 'was' the Word etc...], which conveys no idea of origin for God or for the Logos, but simply continuous existence, "I am."*

Quite a different verb **egeneto**, *"became," appears in John 1:14 for the beginning of the Incarnation of the Logos. The Word 'became' flesh.* **The incarnation is not the origin of Jesus.** *See the distinction sharply drawn in* **John 8:58,** *"before Abraham was [born,* **genesthai** *from* **ginomai - to become**], *I am." The word* **eimi**, *I am; the essence of being, suggesting timeless existence. See also John 1:15, John the Baptists said, "He was, before I was born."*

1 Peter 1:16 On the very account that what is [1]written in prophetic Scripture, *[and echoed in your innermost being],* **already mirrors the life of your design, you are free to [2]be who you are. As it is written, "I am, therefore you are. I am wholly separated unto you, and invite you to explore the same completeness of your being in me."**

[1] The word, [1]grapho, to engrave, often refers to the prophetic writings, Old Testament Scripture. The appeal of truth is confirmed in the resonance within us due to the echo of that which is already written in our innermost being by design. "Did not our hearts ignite within us while he opened to us the Scriptures. Luke 24:27,32,44,45.

[2] The Textus Receptus [KJV] uses the word **genesthe**, *from* **ginomai**, *to become; instead of [2]esesthe, from* **eimi**, *I am, as in the Westtcott & Hort text. This makes a massive difference.*

You did not begin in your mother's womb. You began in God's I-amness. You are the most magnificent idea that the Engineer of the Universe has ever had. **I knew you before I formed you in your mother's womb. Jeremiah 1:5.**

In him we live and move and have our being; we are indeed his offspring! Acts 17:28.

Sonship and Innocence Redeemed

Hebrews 1:1 Throughout [1]ancient times God spoke in many fragments and glimpses of prophetic thought to our fathers. Now, this entire conversation has [2]finally dawned in sonship. Suddenly, what seemed to be an ancient language falls fresh and new like the dew on the tender grass. He is the sum total of every utterance of God. He is whom the Prophets pointed to and we are his immediate audience. *(The word [1]palai, meaning, of old, ancient; from* **palin** *through the idea of oscillatory repetition or retrocession; anew, afresh. Like in James 1:24, we have forgotten what* *manner of people we are - we have forgotten the face of our birth. Jesus successfully rescued the real you, not the pseudo, make-belief you. God has never believed less of you than what he was able to communicate in the sonship that Jesus mirrored and redeemed.*

The word [2]eschatos means extreme; last in time or in space; the uttermost part, the final conclusion. What God said about 'you-manity' in Jesus defines eschatology.)

Hebrews 1:2 In a son, God declares the Incarnate Word to be the heir of all things. He is, after all, the author of the ages.

Hebrews 1:3 The Messiah-message is what has been on the tip of the Father's tongue all along. Now he is the crescendo of God's conversation with us and gives context and content to the authentic, prophetic thought. Everything that God has in mind for mankind is voiced in him. Jesus is God's language. He is the [1]radiant and flawless mirror expression of the person of God. He makes the [2]glorious intent of God visible and exhibits the [3]character and every attribute of Elohim in human form. His being announces our redeemed innocence; having accomplished purification for sins, he sat down, enthroned in the boundless measure of his majesty in the right and of God as his executive authority. He is the force of the universe, [4]upholding everything that exists. This conversation is the dynamic that sustains the entire cosmos. *(The word απαυγασμα [1]apaugasma, only occurs here, and once only in the Greek Septuagint, LXX, in the book of Wisdom 7:26, "For she is the brightness of the everlasting light, the unspotted mirror of the power of God, and the image of his goodness." [The book of Wisdom 7:26.] The word, δόξα [2]doxa glory is the expression of the divine attributes collectively. It is the unfolded fullness of the divine perfections. Vincent. The word χαρακτηρ [3]charakter from χάραγμα charagma - to engrave - translated "mark" of the beast, in Revelation 13:16,17. Either the character of the Father or the character of the fallen mind will influence our actions (hand) because it is what engages our thoughts (forehead).*

"Having accomplished purification of sins, he sat down ..." His *throne is the very endorsement of mankind's redeemed innocence. See Eph 1:20-23; LXX Ps 109:1.*

The words, φέρων τε τὰ πάντα - [4]upholding all things, are not static, but "They imply sustaining, but also movement. It deals with a burden, not as a dead weight, but as in continual movement; as Weiss puts it, "with the all in all its changes and transformations throughout the aeons." Vincent.

More than two thousand years ago the conversation that had begun before time was recorded—sustained in fragments of thought throughout the ages, whispered in prophetic language, chiselled in stone and inscribed in human conscience and memory — became a man. Beyond the tablet of stone, the papyrus scroll or parchment roll, human life has become the articulate voice of God. Jesus is the crescendo of God's conversation with mankind; he gives context and content to the authentic thought. His name declares his mission. As Savior of the world he truly redeemed the image and likeness of the invisible God and made him apparent again in human form as in a mirror.)

1 Peter 1:19 but you were redeemed with the priceless blood of Christ. He is the ultimate sacrifice; spotless and without blemish. Jesus completes the prophetic picture.

In him God speaks the most radical scapegoat language of the law of judgment and brings final closure to a dead and redundant system.

*In **Psalm 40:6,7**, it is clearly stated that God does not require sacrifices or offerings. Jesus is the Lamb of God. He collides victoriously with the futile sacrificial system whereby offerings are constantly made to the pseudo, moody, monster gods of our imagination. This is the scandal of the cross. God does not demand a sacrifice that would change the way he thinks about mankind; he provides the sacrifice of himself in Christ in order to forever eradicate sin-consciousness from our minds and radically change the way we think about our Maker, one another and ourselves.*

Sin is singular - its symptoms are plural - its been a sonship thing from the beginning - no wonder Jesus says freedom indeed is found in the truth of our authentic and redeemed sonship - even the "other brother" has the Father pleading with him, "My son you have always been with me and all that I have is yours!!" Sin is not about things you do or don't do - sin is missing out on sonship!

It was God's initiative from start to finish

Romans 4:1 If we look at our father Abraham as an example and scrutinize his life, would you say that he discovered any reason for placing confidence in the flesh through personal contribution?

Romans 4:2 If he felt that his friendship with God was a reward for good behavior, then surely he would have reason to recommend the recipe; yet it is plain to see that it was all God's initiative from start to finish.

Romans 4:3 Scripture is clear, Abraham reflected God's belief in him; this is the basis of the [1]rediscovery of [2]righteousness.

([1] [1]One must remember that in Adam & Eve's communion with Elohim, something was lost which would be redeemed - there would be a "return" to the consciousness of this union.

[2] *2This most significant, relational term, righteousness, points to a shared likeness; this includes one's authentic identity and innocence.*

The word 2dikaiosune, righteousness is from the stem dike, two parties finding likeness in each other. Also, note that the name of the Greek goddess of Justice is Dike [pronounced, Dikey]; she is always pictured holding a scale of balances in her hand.)

This thought is powerfully emphasized in Abram's encounter with Melchizedek in Genesis 14, on the threshold of Genesis 15 where God cuts covenant with Abraham and introduces him to righteousness based on faith, and not one's natural lineage, heritage or performance.

Who am I?

In **Mirror-language**, Jesus asks the most important, two-in-one question, in Matthew 16:13, **Who is the son of man? Who am I?** In this question, Jesus mirror-echoes the universal quest of the human race.

Upon the rock of this revelation, that the son of man is the son of God, he builds his ekklesia, *[authentic identity]* and the gates of the blindfold-mode *[hades; ha, not and eido, to see]* will not prevail against it! See Rev 1:18;

also, **Rev 3:7 And to the messenger of the ekklesia of Philadelphia write: I am the Holy and True One. I hold the key of David as prophesied in Isaiah 22:22. Yes, I unlock the mysteries of the heavenly dimension and no one can shut the door. And I lock the entrance and none of the old mindsets can access it.**

"Simon, son of Jonah, flesh and blood did not reveal this to you! Now that you know who I am, allow me to introduce you to you, Mr Rock! *[Petros]* You're a chip of the old Block! *[Petra]*

See Isaiah 51:1,2 and Deuteronomy 18:4,18. Also my extended notes at the end of Revelation 2. https://www.mirrorword.net/books/revelation-the-apocalypse-uncovered-msb

The younger biological brother of Jesus, James, like his other siblings, did not believe that their brother was indeed the Messiah...

John 7:5 Yet none of his immediate family believed that he really was the Christ. It was only after his resurrection when Jesus also appeared to James, that his brother's eyes were opened, *1 Corinthians 15:7, and Galatians 1:19.* This prompted James to write about seeing the face of your birth when you hear the authentic word of our co-begotteness by the Father of lights. *James 1:17,23.*

James 1:17 Without exception God's [1]gifts are only good; its perfection cannot be flawed. They come from [2]above *(where we originate from)*; proceeding like light rays from its source, the Father of lights, with whom there is no distortion, or even a shadow of shifting to obstruct, or intercept the light; nor any hint of a hidden agenda.

[1] The principle of a [1]gift, puts "reward-language" out of business.

[2] The word, [2]anouthen, means, from above. John 3:3, 13.

James 1:18 We are God's idea to begin with! Our true origin is preserved in God's resolve. It was according to the Father's delight that he birthed us; giving authentic, incarnate expression to the Word. *[The face to face-ness of the Logos that was before time was. John 1:1]* Just like the first-fruits mirror the harvest, so we mirror the conclusion of his workmanship in the core of our being.

James 1:23 Anyone who hears the word, sees the face of their birth, as in a mirror. The difference between a mere spectator and a participator is that both of them hear the same voice and perceive in its message the face of their own genesis reflected there;

James 1:24 they realize that they are looking at themselves, but for the one it seems just too good to be true; this person departs *[back to the old way of seeing themselves]*, and immediately forgets what manner of person they are; never giving another thought to the one they saw there in the mirror.

James 1:25 The other is [1]mesmerized by what they see; [2]captivated by the effect of a law that frees them from the obligation to the old written code that restricted them to their own efforts and willpower. No distraction or contradiction can dim the impact of what is seen in the mirror concerning the law of perfect [3]liberty *[the law of faith]* that now frees one to get on with the act of living the life *[of their original design.]* They find a new [3]spontaneous lifestyle; the poetry of practical living.

Romans 8:29, He pre-designed and engineered us from the start to be jointly fashioned in the same mold and image of his Son according to the exact blueprint of his thought. We see the original and intended pattern of our lives preserved in his Son. He is the firstborn from the same womb that reveals our genesis. He confirms that we are the invention of God. Also, John 1:1-18; 1 Pet. 2:9,10.

John 1:13 These are the ones who discover their genesis in God, beyond their natural conception. This is not about our blood lineage or whether we were a wanted- or unwanted-child; this is about our God-begotteness. We are his dream come true and not the invention of our parents. You are indeed the greatest idea that God has ever had. *[See Jeremiah 1:5; 29:11 & John 3:2-7]*

Also 2 Corinthians 3:18 Now, we all, with new understanding, see ourselves in him as in a mirror... We suddenly realize that we are looking into a mirror, where every feature of his image, articulated in Christ, is reflected within us. The Spirit of the Lord engineers this radical transformation; we are led from an inferior mind-set to the revealed endorsement of our authentic identity. From the fading glory of our own making, to the discovering of the most amazing reality, that we are his glory! *(We've got our masks off and God's brilliance is bouncing off our faces. We're glowing from knowing. 2 Cor. 3:18 [Rob Lacey]*

Abraham saw My Day

Genesis 22:7 Then Isaac said to Abraham, My father; and he said, Here am I, my son. And he said, We have wood and fire here, but where is the lamb for the burnt offering?

Genesis 22:13 And Abraham lifted up his eyes and looked. And behold! A ram <u>behind him</u> was entangled in a thicket by its horns. And Abraham went and took the ram and offered it for a burnt offering instead of his son. *(This reminds of **Revelation 1:10** I was in a spiritual trance where I witnessed the [1]Day of the Lord. I heard a loud voice [2]behind me, clear and distinct, like the sound of a trumpet. (The [1]Day of the Lord is the very day to which the prophetic voice of the Spirit of Christ pointed - Jesus the Messiah, is the fulfillment of this day. The word [2]opiso points to that which is behind in place and time. The fact that John hears a word **behind him** is so significant. It means that what he hears already happened within its prophetic context.*

Genesis 22:14 And Abraham called the name of that place Jaweh Sees; so that it is said until this day, "In the mount of Jaweh, it will be seen!" יהוה יראה *Jaweh Jireh Jaweh sees!*

Genesis 22:17 that blessing I will bless you, and multiplying I will multiply your seed as the stars of the heavens, and as the sand which is on the shore of the sea. And your Seed shall possess the gate of His enemies.

Genesis 22:18 And in your Seed shall all the nations of the earth be blessed.

John 8:56 Your father Abraham was leaping with joy to see my day. What he saw made him exceedingly glad.

John Then the Jews said, "Ha. You're not even fifty years old and you claim to have seen Abraham."

John 8:58 "Most certainly do I say unto you that before Abraham was born, I am." *("Before Abraham was [born, **genesthai** from **ginomai** - to become] I am." The word **eimi**, I am; the essence of being, suggesting timeless existence.)*

Slave or Son?

Jacob, the son of Isaac...

Luke 3:34 son of Jacob, son of Isaac, son of Abraham, son of Terah, son of Nahor, *(The name, יעקב Jacob means, the heel-holder. Hosea 12:3 In the womb he took his brother by the heel, And by his strength he was a prince with God.*

Also, **Genesis 25:23 And the Lord said to her, "Two nations are in your womb, and the two peoples, born of you, shall be divided; the one shall be stronger than the other; the elder shall serve the younger."**

> *The two come out of the same mold; yet they represent two types of people: one who understands their true identity by faith [authentic value] and one who seeks to identify themselves after the flesh [performance-based].*

> *Again, the law of performance versus the law of faith is emphasized in order to prepare the ground for the promise-principle.*

> *Mankind's salvation would be by promise and not by performance; i.e. it would not be a reward for good behavior. No one will be justified by the tree of the knowledge of good and evil; **poneros**, "evil," full of hardships, annoyances and labor. The Tree of Life is our true "Family-tree".*

Galatians 3:6 Abraham had no other claim to righteousness but simply believing what God declared concerning him. Isaac confirmed God's faith, not Abraham's efforts. This is all we have in common with Abraham.

Galatians 3:7 The conclusion is clear; faith and not flesh relates us to Abraham. *(Grace rather than law is our true lineage. Ishmael represents so much more than the Muslim religion. Ishmael represents the clumsy effort of the flesh to compete with faith; the preaching of a mixed message of law and grace.)*

John 8:32 In this abiding you will fully know the truth about who you are and this knowing will be your freedom.

John 8:33 They answered him, "We are the seed of Abraham; we have never been anybody's slaves. Why do you suggest that we are not free?"

John 8:34 Jesus answered and said, "I say unto you with absolute certainty that everyone engaging in the distorted mindset of sin is a slave to it." *(Sin is not about things you do or don't do - sin is missing out on sonship. Their failing to see Jesus as their Messiah, and him as the mirror image Redeemer of their true sonship, is their sin. Religion is enslaved to the fruit of the wrong tree.*

The sin-system is governed by the idea of justification by personal effort, performance and pretense; which is the typical fruit of the 'I am-not-mind-set' which Peter refers to as the futile ways we inherited from our fathers. 1 Peter 1:18.)

John 8:35 The difference between the slave and the son is that the slave only works there; for the son the father's house is home.

John 8:36 With the freedom found in sonship there is [1]no pretense. *(Free indeed. The word, [1]ontoos, indeed is the opposite to what is pretended.)*

Galatians 4:22 The law records the fact that Abraham had two sons: one by a slave girl, the other by a free woman.

Galatians 4:23 The one is produced by the flesh *[the Do It Yourself-tree]*, **the other by faith** *[the promise]*.

Galatians 4:24 There is a parallel meaning in the story of the two sons: they represent two systems, works and grace.

Galatians 4:25 Sinai is an Arabian rocky mountain named after Hagar, *[outside the land of promise]*. **Its association with the law of Moses mirrors Jerusalem as the capital of Jewish legalism. Hagar is the mother of the law of works.** *[DIY-religion "Do it Yourself"]*

Galatians 4:26 But <u>the mother from above</u>, the true mother of mankind is grace, the free Jerusalem; she is the mother of the promise.

Galatians 4:27 For it is written, "Rejoice, Oh childless one. Erupt in jubilee. For though you have never known travail before, your children will greatly outnumber her who was married." *(Married to the law; Isaiah 54:1; see also Romans 7:1-6.)*

Galatians 4:28 We resemble Isaac: we are begotten of faith; the promise is our parent.

Galatians 4:29 Just as when the flesh child persecuted the faith child, so now these Jerusalem Jews in their Christian disguise seek to harass you;

Galatians 4:30 however, Scripture is clear: "Expel the slave mother and her son; the slave son cannot inherit with the free son."

(In exactly the same way, rid your minds radically from the slave mother and child mentality. Light dispels darkness effortlessly.)

Galatians 4:31 Realize whose children we are my Brothers and Sisters: we are not children of the slave-mother, the law, but children of the free mother; we are begotten of grace.

The symbolic nature of circumcision is further emphasized here,

See **Deuteronomy 10:16, Circumcise therefore the foreskin of your heart, and be no longer stubborn.**

Romans 4:10 So, the question is, was he reckoned righteous before or after he was circumcised? It is clear that Abraham's faith-encounters *[as recorded in Genesis 12 through 15]*, **happened long before circumcision was mentioned!** *(The symbolic circumcision covenant was only introduced years later in Genesis 17, when he was already 99 years old. [Isaac's birth is only recorded in Genesis 21.])*

Romans 4:11 Thus, Abraham received circumcision as an external, symbolic [1]seal to remind him of what God has already [2]declared many years ago, when he was first introduced to the concept of "the [3]righteousness of God". Since Abraham's supernatural fatherhood is celebrated in circumcision, it infers that he is both the father of Jew and Gentile alike - God already engaged him in covenant as an uncircumcised Gentile - he thus represents them in all that was predicted concerning the blessing of every nation in the Seed of faith!

([1] A [1]seal of the righteousness of the faith - **sphragida tēs dikaiosunēs tēs pisteōs***. The [1]seal of circumcision, was not meant to be a distraction but rather a prophetic confirmation to the only valid basis to "the righteousness [of God]" by the principle of the faith [of God].*

Just like a receipt is only a reference to, and not the actual transaction. Note, the *faith and* the *righteousness. See 2 Corinthians 13:5. Also here in Romans 4:25.*

[2] Circumcision did not introduce an adjusted or new covenant - it was simply added as a symbolic seal in [2]confirmation to God's resolve, as recorded in Genesis 12:2,3 and Genesis 15:5.

In the meantime, Abraham's moments of unbelief, delays and detours did not distract from God's determined destiny for the prophetic Messianic Seed.

Galatians 3:16 It is on record that the promise *[of the blessing of righteousness by God's faith]* **was made to Abraham and to his seed, singular,** *[thus excluding his effort to produce Ishmael.]* **Isaac, the child of promise, and not of the flesh, mirrors the Messiah.** *[Genesis 3:15]*

Galatians 5:11 Would I compromise the message of the cross and preach circumcision just to avoid persecution. How insane would that be? *(This whole matter boils down to thinking that justification is the result of something we still have to do, or knowing that it is the result of something that God has already done.)*

Galatians 5:12 These people who are so keen to cut off things should ¹chop off their legalistic influence in your lives altogether. *(ἀποκόπτω apokoptō with Preposition, apo, away from, and kopto, to chop off, mutilate/dismember/castrate)*

Just as Paul's noble birth was not his claim to fame - **God separated me from my mother's womb! Grace defines me! Not my natural lineage and identity as son of Benjamin. Galatians 1:15.**

John 7:22 Lets take one of those rules: Moses represents circumcision as the tradition of the fathers and you are okay with performing the cut on the Sabbath;

John 7:23 now in order not to disappoint Moses you have made your circumcision rule superior to the Sabbath; when a boy is eight days old you have no problem with performing circumcision even when it coincides with the Sabbath and here I am making a man's entire body well on the Sabbath and you're ready to kill me and break another one of the ten commandments. *(See Genesis 17:12, "He that is eight days old among you shall be circumcised.")*

John 7:24 Do not cloud righteous judgment with your biased opinions and traditions."

There is no "magical power" in circumcision

Romans 2:25 The real value of circumcision is tested by your ability to keep the law. If you break the law you might as well not be circumcised.

Romans 2:26 The fact that you are circumcised does not distinguish you from the rest of the world; it does not give you super-human power to keep the commandments.

Romans 2:27 If it is not about who is circumcised or not, but rather who keeps the law or not, then in that case even uncircumcised people can judge the ones who claim to know it all and have it all. On the one hand you have those who feel naturally inclined to do what is right, yet none of them are circumcised, then you have the circumcised who know the letter of the law but fail to keep it.

Romans 2:28 So it is not about who you appear to be on the outside that makes you a real Jew, but who you really are on the inside.

Romans 2:29 For you to know who you are in your heart is the secret of your spirit identity; this is your true circumcision, it is not the literal outward appearance that distinguishes you. After all it is God's approval and not another's opinion that matters most. People see skin-deep; God knows the heart.

1 Corinthians 7:18 Circumcision or the lack of it does not [1]define you. In Christ your Jewish or Gentile heritage is irrelevant and can never again [1]label you. *(The word, [1]kaleo, means to identify by name; to surname.)*

1 Corinthians 7:19 You couldn't keep the commandments anyway, whether you were circumcised or not. *(So if circumcision did not contribute anything while you were seeking to be justified under the law, how can it possibly now advantage you in your understanding of righteousness by faith?)*

Circumcision controversy

Galatians 2:2 I especially wanted the most senior leadership of the church to hear what I teach in the Gentile nations as my revelation and specific emphasis of the Gospel. We decided to meet in private to avoid any possible public controversy. In this way they could best judge for themselves whether, according to their opinion, my ministry had credibility or not.

Galatians 2:3 Our Greek companion, Titus, survived the circumcision scrutiny and wasn't forced to go for the cut.

Galatians 5:1 Christ defines your faith; he is your freedom from anything from which the law could never free you. Find your firm footing in this freedom. Do not let religion trip you up again and harness you to a system of rules and obligations. *(In this parallel, Christ represents Sarah, the faith-mother who birthed you in the resurrection. The rock-hewn tomb represents Sarah's dead womb. 1 Pet 1:3.)*

Galatians 5:2 I, Paul, am of the opinion, and you can quote me: If you would again consider circumcision as necessary to improve your standing before God, then you make Christ of no relevance to yourselves. Then you might as well delete him from your life altogether. *(By still holding on to any Jewish sentiment like keeping the Sabbath, etc, has the same effect.)*

Galatians 5:3 I will state it categorically, that if you endorse circumcision as a means to obtain righteousness, you are immediately obliged to keep the whole law. *(In for a penny, in for a pound.)*

Galatians 5:4 Law-righteousness has nothing in common with grace-righteousness; they are opposites. As impossible as it is for anyone to travel in two opposite directions at the same time, equally irrelevant Christ becomes to anyone who continues to pursue righteousness under the law.

Galatians 5:5 Our minds are made up; there is absolutely no advantage for anyone to pursue righteousness in the flesh; righteousness is a spirit dimension reality and can only be [1]embraced by faith. What God believes is our exclusive reference. *(Any other basis for righteousness leaves mankind falling hopelessly short. The word, [1]apekdechomai is often translated, to wait for; the components however, point to a favorable embrace; apo, from, ek out of, and dechomai to grasp, to welcome hospitably, to embrace.)*

Galatians 5:6 God believes that we are fully represented in Christ, which takes circumcision or any contribution of the flesh out of the equation. Love fuels belief and sets faith in motion. *(It is easy for love to believe.)*

Galatians 5:7 You started off like an athlete on a mission, who distracted you? You seemed so completely persuaded about the truth.

Galatians 5:8 God is not confused about you. He surnamed you.

Galatians 5:9 It is impossible to hide the effect of the smallest amount of yeast; the process of fermentation is immediately triggered. *(A little bit of legalism corrupts a person's whole life.)*

Galatians 6:14 May my boasting be in nothing but the cross of our Lord Jesus Christ, through whom the world has been crucified to me and I to the world. The religious-systems and applause of this world have no appeal to me. As far as they are concerned, I am like a dead person.

Galatians 6:15 The new creation in Christ steals the show; not whether someone is circumcised or not. *(God associated us in Christ; when he died we died, when he was raised we were raised together with him in newness of life.)*

Galatians 6:16 Our union with Christ sets the pace and makes us the true Israel, not whether we are Jew or Gentile, circumcised or not. Oh, what peace we discover in his mercy. This rule is the new law we submit ourselves to as the principle of our daily walk.

Galatians 6:17 I will not be troubled anymore. I already bear enough scars in my body that brand me as being under the ownership of Jesus. *(Those scars that I carry from being persecuted for this Gospel are more significant to me than the scar of circumcision.)*

Ephesians 2:11 Remember where you came from; [not only were you spiritually dead but] it wasn't long ago when you were still classified as non-Jewish, judging on the surface you had nothing that linked you to them. They sneered at you because you didn't share their distinguishing mark of circumcision, which was their claim to fame.

Ephesians 2:12 During that time you were distanced from the Messianic hope; you had nothing in common with Israel. You felt foreign to the covenants of prophetic promise, living a life with nothing to look forward to in a world where God seemed absent.

Ephesians 2:13 But now, wow. Everything has changed; you have discovered yourselves to be located in Christ. What once seemed so distant is now so near; his blood reveals your redeemed innocence and authentic genesis.

Ephesians 2:14 It is in him that we are one and at peace with everyone; he dissolved every definition of division. (What we know will put war and divorce out of business.)

Ephesians 2:15 In his incarnation, he rendered the entire Jewish system of ceremonial laws and regulations useless as a measure to justify human life and conduct. In that he died mankind's death all grounds for tension and hostility were entirely removed. The peace he proclaims reveals one new human race, created and defined in Christ, instead of two groups of people separated by their ethnic identity and differences.

Ephesians 2:16 Both parties are fully represented and equally reconciled to God in one human body through the cross. He reinstated the former harmony; all opposing elements were thus utterly defeated.

Ephesians 2:17 On that basis he made his public appearance, proclaiming the Good News of peace to the entire human race; both those who felt left out in the cold [as far as the promises and covenants were concerned], as well as to those who were near all along [because of their Jewish identity].

Ephesians 2:18 Because of Christ both Jew and Gentile now enjoy equal access to the Father in one Spirit.

Ephesians 2:19 The conclusion is clear; you are no longer frowned upon as a foreigner; you are where you belong and part of an intimate family.

Brood of Vipers

In Luke 3:7 John the baptist calls the people an [1]offspring of serpents!

Brood of Vipers - [1]*begotten of a mindset, poisoned by the serpent that snared mankind in the garden of Eden and abandoned them in the wilderness of a lost identity.*

John 8:37 I know you are the seed of Abraham, yet you are seeking opportunity to kill me because my word finds no [1]resonance in you. *(The word χορός - choros relates to a* [1]*chorus, harmony in song or dance.)*

John 8:38 I observe my Father's voice with close attention; this inspires my every expression. You hear a different father's voice and behave accordingly.

John 8:39 They immediately responded with, "But Abraham is our father." To which Jesus replied, "If you were conceived by Abraham's faith, you would mirror his persuasion. *(Jesus said in John 6:29 This is the work of God; your belief in the One whom he has sent.)*

John 8:40 But here you are, desiring to destroy me because I declare to you the truth which I heard from a place of intimate acquaintance with God; this certainly does not reflect Abraham's faith.

John 8:41 Your actions clearly show who your father is." They said unto him, "We are not conceived in fornication, God is our only Father."

John 8:42 Jesus said, "If you were convinced that God was your Father, you would love me. Look, here I am. I did not arrive here by my own doing; I proceeded from him who sent me.

John 8:43 You do not understand my [1]language because you do not hear my logic. *(My dialect seems foreign to you because you are not familiar with the Logic of God. You might be acquainted with the letter of the law in Scripture but you are not acquainted with the Word. See John 5:39,40 also John 8:31. The word* [1]*lalia means dialect or language.)*

John 8:44 You are the offspring of a perverse mindset and you prove its [1]diabolical parenthood in your willingness to execute its cravings. The intention was to [2]murder humanity's awareness of their god-identity [3]from the beginning since it is in violent opposition to the idea of the image and likeness of God in human form. It cannot abide the truth. Lying is the typical [4]language of the distorted desire of the father of deception. *(The word,* [1]*diabolos, Devil, has two components, **dia**, because of, or through and **ballo**, to cast down; thus referring a cast down condition and warped mentality that mankind inherited in their association with Adam's fall.*

The diabolos is a man-slayer, [2]**anthrōpoktonos** *from* **anthropos** *and* **kteinoo** *to kill. The word for the human species, male or female is* **anthropos***, from* **ana***, upward, and* **tropos***, manner of life; character; in* *like manner. See John 1:51, 2:25. [3]Just like Eve was deceived to believe a lie about herself, which is the fruit of the "I-am-not-tree". The word [4]lalia means dialect or language.*

<u>Your True Circumcision!</u>

Luke 3:8 [1]**Now,** [2]**bear fruit that matches the** [3]**awakening of your authentic identity and your redeemed innocence. Quit seeking your origin in Abraham - your true lineage is found in God's faith; not in Abraham's efforts to bear children. See beyond mere flesh and discover God's power** [4]**raising the offspring of Abraham out of these stones.**

([1] Again, the [1]Aorist Imperative is used; ποιησατε from [1]poieoo, "Get on with it." Stressing the urgency and priority of the matter.

[2 & 3] [2]Let this [3]metanoia-moment conceive your offspring. Cease bearing the viper-fruit of a lost identity. [See notes on Luke 3:3]

[4] The word εγειραι [4]egeirai, from egeiroo, to arouse from sleep; to raise the dead. Here in the Aorist Infinitive which presents the action expressed by the verb as a completed unit with a beginning and end. In this parallel, Christ represents Sarah, the faith-mother who re-birthed you in the resurrection. The rock-hewn tomb represents Sarah's dead womb. 1 Peter 1:3. See Deut. 32:18, "You were unmindful of the Rock that begot you, and you forgot the God who gave you birth..

I love John the Baptist's father, Zechariah's song recorded in Luke 1 ... here is just a glimpse...

Luke 1:73 As in the face to face oath which he gave to Abraham our father.

Luke 1:74 This was his resolve and gift to us all along - he undertook to rescue us out of the grip of everything contrary to us, freeing us to worship him without fear,

Luke 1:75 in [1]**spontaneous innocence and righteousness, every day of our lives.** *The word, ὁσιότης hosiotēs suggests an innocence beyond the written code.*

Colossians 2:11 You were in Christ when he died; which means that his death is your true circumcision. This is [1]**not hypothetical; this is the real deal. Thus, sin's authority in the human body was stripped of its control over you.** *(ἀχειροποίητος [1]acheiro-poiētos; meaning, not made with hands.)*

Colossians 2:12 In the same parallel *[your co-circumcision in his death]*, **your co-burial and joint-resurrection is now demonstrated in baptism; your co-inclusion in Christ is what God's faith knew when he powerfully raised him from the dead.** *(Hosea 6:2.)*

He is the Desire of the Nations

John 12:19 The Pharisees were perplexed about this and said, "Look, we are gaining no ground against him. The entire world is running after him."

John 12:20 There were also a number of Greeks who came to worship at the feast because of the rumors they have heard.

John 12:21 They approached Phillip who was from Bethsaida in Galilee and asked him, "Sir, we would be delighted to see Jesus. Is there perhaps any chance that you could introduce us to him?" *(He had a Greek name and the Greeks may have seen Philip in Galilee where there were many Greeks.)*

John 12:22 Phillip went and told Andrew and the two of them told Jesus.

John 12:23 Jesus, immediately understanding the prophetic significance of the moment, knew that he, the Messiah, was who all the nations were longing for and answered, "The hour is here for the Son of man to be glorified.** *(Jesus studied Scripture as in a mirror - he knew that "in the book, it is written about me." Haggai 2:7 and the desire of the nations shall come...See Col 1:27.)*

John 12:24 Most certainly shall the single grain of wheat fall into the earth and die - if it doesn't die it remains alone - but in its death it produces much fruit.

Your word saturates the earth of hardened hearts and minds, to then extend that the hidden mystery within the incorruptible seed, germinates and sprouts, and bears much fruit!

Isaiah 55:10,11 "For as the rain and the snow come down from heaven, and return not there without saturating the earth [all flesh], so shall my word be that goes forth from my mouth; it shall not return to me empty, but it shall accomplish that which I purpose, and prosper in the thing for which I sent it.**

In him every definition of separation and distance is canceled. The prophetic word was destined to become flesh; every nook and cranny of human life is saturated in the incarnation.

"And in your Seed shall all the nations of the earth be blessed!"

John 12:25 To hold on desperately to a mere life defined by the soul realm is to lose it; but to abandon the soul substitute for the real deal is to observe your spiritual life which is the life of the ages.**

While sin means missing out on sonship; righteousness and redemption is a celebration of sonship!

"Can these bones live?"

One wonders why God showed Ezekiel a valley of bleached bones? There is Zero sign of life left! And then asks the question, "Can these bones live?" Ezekiel 37

And why God waited till Sarah's womb was dead!

And why God only created Adam on the 6th day when all his work was already done? No help needed from Adam!

Jesus didn't die 99% or for 99% - He died humanity's death 100%

"The love of Christ constrains me because I am convinced that if one has died for all, then all died!" If Paul had to compromise the last part of verse 14 of 2 Corinthians 5 to read: "One has died for all therefore only those who follow the prescriptions to qualify, have also died," then he would have had to change the first half of the verse as well!

Only the love of Christ can make a calculation of such enormous proportions!

How can we underestimate such a great salvation!

The good news unveils the love of God spectacularly! And the dimensions of his love exceed any concept we could possibly have of length or breadth, *(the horizontal extent of agape which includes the entire planet)* - neither the depth of darkness and hell he descended to nor the heights of heaven he raised us to!

Something happened to mankind, **while we were still dead in our trespasses and sins!** We were co-quickened and co raised without our permission! Ephesians 2:5,6

Romans 4:23 Here is the Good News: the recorded words, "It was reckoned to him" were not written for his sake alone.

Romans 4:24 Scripture was written with us in mind. We are audience to the same faith in the face of death. The same [1]conclusion is now equally relevant in our realizing the significance of Jesus' resurrection from the dead.

(By raising Jesus from the dead God proclaims our redeemed innocence.

Isaac's birth from Sarah's barren womb prophetically declared the resurrection of Jesus from the tomb. Abraham's best efforts could not produce Isaac. Sarah's dead womb is a picture of the impossibility of the flesh to produce a child.

This underlines mankind's inability to redeem themselves under the performance-based law of willpower.

Jesus said, "Abraham saw my day." Mankind's most extreme self-sacrifice offered in an attempt to win the favorable attention of their deity could never match the sacrifice of God's Lamb to win the attention of mankind.

Faith sees the future in past tense-mode.

The resurrection is the ultimate proof and trophy of righteousness by God's faith. [See Rom 6:11] **[1]logitsomai** *- logical conclusion. "Consider [**logitsomai**] yourself dead indeed," compared with Romans 4:19, "Abraham considered his own body dead." We can only study Scripture in the context of Christ as representing the human race; God had us in mind all along [John 5:39].)*

Romans 4:25 While our sins resulted in his death; our righteousness and redeemed innocence is celebrated in his resurrection!

(It is most wonderful to discover that his resurrection does not include us only once we believe!

*Paul uses the word, **dia** twice in this verse! Unfortunately most translations in most languages only translate the 1st **dia** correctly!*

He was handed over <u>BECAUSE of</u> *[**dia**] our sins - why was he raised?*

NOT so that some small portion of the "elite christian group" may stand a dim chance to be justified!!!

*NO! Hallelujah! The same word, **dia** is used again!*

He was raised <u>BECAUSE of</u> *[**dia**] our righteousness!*

His cross = our sins,

His resurrection = our innocence.

Romans 4:3 Scripture is clear, Abraham reflected God's belief in him; this is the basis of the [1]rediscovery of [2]righteousness.

([1] [1]One must remember that in Adam & Eve's communion with Elohim, something was lost which would be redeemed - there would be a "return" to the consciousness of this union.

[2] [2]This most significant, relational term, righteousness, points to a shared likeness; this includes one's authentic identity and innocence.

*The word [2]**dikaiosune**, righteousness is from the stem **dike**, two parties finding likeness in each other.*

Also, note that the name of the Greek goddess of Justice is Dike [pronounced, Dikey]; she is always pictured holding a scale of balances in her hand.)

5:1 The [1]conclusion is clear: our blameless innocence has absolutely nothing to do with something we did to qualify ourselves; it is what happened to us, solely because of our Lord Jesus Christ's doing. Faith, and not reward, is the only valid [2]basis for righteousness. Let us now fully [2]engage this seamless union in our [3]face to face [4]friendship with God. *(In one sentence Paul sums up the previous four chapters. "Standing then acquitted as the result of faith, let us enjoy peace with God through our Lord Jesus Christ." Weymouth NT. The word [1]dikaiothentes is an Aorist Participle, which translates, "having been justified by faith." See previous verse, Rom 4:25 "...who was delivered up because of our offences, and was raised up because of our being declared righteous." Young's Literal Translation. The Preposition [2]ek confirms that faith is the source or basis of our righteousness. Let us have [[2]echo, engage/resonate] peace with God - eirēnēn echōmen pros ton theon. This is the correct text beyond a doubt, the Present Active Subjunctive, <u>not</u> echomen (Present Indicative) of the Textus Receptus. One has only to observe the force of the tense to see Paul's meaning clearly. The mode is the volitive subjunctive and the Present tense expresses linear action. [Robertson] The Preposition [3]pros means face to face; see John 1:1. The word, [4]eirene, means peace, from eiro, to join, to be set at one again, in carpentry it is referred to as the dove-tail joint, which is the strongest joint. Peace is a place of unhindered enjoyment of friendship beyond guilt, suspicion, blame or inferiority.)*

5:2 Jesus is God's face to face grace [1]embrace of the entire human race. So here we are, [2]standing tall in the joyful bliss of our redeemed innocence! We are God's [3]dream come true! This was God's [4]idea all along! *(To be welcomed with wide-open arms, [1]prosagoge, from pros, face to face and ago, to lead as a shepherd leads his sheep. The words, 'by faith' are in brackets in the Greek text and are not supported by the best Greek manuscripts. Joy is not an occasional happy feeling; we are [2]positioned there, [2]histemi, in an immovable, unthreatened union! Hope, [2]elpis from elpo, to anticipate, usually with pleasure. The word [4]doxa, often translated, glory, is from dokeo, to form an idea, opinion.)*

5:3 Our blissful boasting in him remains uninterrupted in times of trouble; we know that pressure reveals patience. Tribulation does not have what it takes to nullify what hope knows we have!

5:4 Patience provides [1]proof of every positive expectation. *([1]dokimos, proof. Thayer Definition: scrutinized and accepted, particularly of coins and money.)*

5:5 This kind of hope does not disappoint; the gift of the Holy Spirit completes our every expectation and ignites the love of God within us like an artesian well. *(ekxeo, to pour out. The Holy Spirit is an outpouring not an in-pouring! See John 7:37-39, also Titus 3:6.)*

5:6 God's timing was absolutely perfect; mankind was at their weakest when Christ died their death. *(We were bankrupt in our efforts to save ourselves.)*

5:7 It is most unlikely that someone will die for another person, even if they are righteous; yet it is remotely possible that someone can brave such devotion that one would actually lay down one's own life in an effort to save the life of an extraordinary good person.

5:8 Herein is the extremity of God's love gift: mankind was rotten to the core when Christ died their death.

5:9 If God could love us that much when we were ungodly and guilty, how much more are we free to realize his love now that we are declared innocent by his blood? *(God does not love us more now that we are reconciled to him; we are now free to realize how much he loved us all along! [Col 2:14, Rom 4:25].)*

5:10 Our hostility and indifference towards God did not reduce his love for us; he saw equal value in us when he exchanged the life of his Son for ours. Now that the act of [1]reconciliation is complete, his life in us saves us from the gutter-most to the uttermost. *(Reconciliation, from [1]katalasso, meaning a mutual exchange of equal value. Thayer Definition: to exchange, as coins for others of equivalent value. "For if while we were enemies we were reconciled to God by the death of his Son, much more, now that we are reconciled, shall we be saved by his life." — RSV.)*

5:11 Thus, our joyful boasting in God continues; Jesus Christ has made reconciliation a reality.

5:12 One person opened the door to [1]sin. Sin introduced *(spiritual)* death. Both sin and death had a global impact. No one escaped its tyranny. *(The word translated sin, is the word [1]hamartia, from ha, negative and meros, portion or form, thus to be without your allotted portion or without form, pointing to a disorientated, distorted identity; the word meros, is the stem of morphe, as in 2 Corinthians 3:18 the word metamorphe, with form, is the opposite of hamartia - without form. Sin is to live out of context with the blueprint of one's design; to behave out of tune with God's original harmony.)*

5:13 The law did not introduce sin; it was just not pointed out yet.

5:14 In the mean time death dominated everyone's lifestyle, from Adam till Moses, *[2500 years before the law was given]* no one was excluded; even those whose sins were different from Adam's. The fact is that Adam's [1]deviation set sin into motion - what happened to mankind because of one man, Adam, is in principle typical of what was about to happen to the same mankind because of the one man, Jesus! *(Paul now employs a word that only he uses in his epistles [7 times]* *parabasis instead of the usual word for sin,* **hamartia** *-* **parabasis** *has two components,* **para**, *which points to a close proximity/union and* **bainos**, *step, footprint - in this sense, a deviation; out of step - out of sync. In Adam mankind became out of sync with their true identity but didn't know it until the law revealed it - in Christ the same mankind became exceedingly righteous, but do not realize it until the gospel reveals it.)*

5:15 The only similarity in the comparison between the ¹crash-landing and the gift, is that both Adam and Christ represent the masses. However, the grace gift lavished upon mankind in the one man Jesus Christ supersedes the effect of Adam's failure by far and is beyond comparison in significance to the idea of ²death and separation. *(Now Paul introduces the word* **¹paraptoma**, *from* **para** *closest possible proximity and* **pipto**, *to descend from a higher place to a lower – to stop flying. No wonder he urges us in Col 3:1-3 to engage our thoughts with the things that are above, where we are co-elevated and jointly enthroned in the heavenlies together with Christ! The word* **²apothnesko**, *death, suggests a separation; from* **apo**, *meaning any kind of separation of one thing from another by which the union or fellowship of the two is destroyed; also of a state of separation and distance. The word,* **thnesko** *means death.*

But God's free gift immeasurably outweighs the transgression. For if through the transgression of the one individual the mass of mankind have died, infinitely greater is the generosity wherewith God's grace, and the gift given in his grace which found expression in the one man Jesus Christ, have been bestowed on the mass of mankind. — Weymouth, 1912.)

5:16 The principle of the gift speaks a different language and brings a radically different equation to the table. Whereas a single sin resulted in a judgment that concluded in condemnation; grace translates countless deviations into acquittal and innocence.

5:17 Death no longer has the final say. Life rules! If the effect of one man's crash-landing engaged mankind in a death-dominated lifestyle how much more advantaged is the very same mankind now that they are the recipients of the boundless reservoirs of grace, empowering them to enjoy the dominion of life through the gift of righteousness because of that one man, Jesus Christ. Grace is out of all proportion in superiority to the transgression. *(No, grace is not something you qualify for by receiving it! Grace already belongs to mankind without their permission! The words* οἱ λαμβάνοντες *-* **¹oi lambanontes** *do not mean, to believingly accept, but simply the recipients! [the Present Active Participle Nominative] The word* **²perisseia** περισσεία *means super abundantly; that which exceeds all boundaries. Of course it doesn't take faith out of the equation! It gives context to faith! See verse 1&2. Faith isn't what you do in order to; it's what happens to you because of!)*

5:18 The conclusion is clear: if one offence condemns the entire human race; then in principle, the righteousness of one vindicates the entire human race. *(Phillips translation: "We see then, that as one act of sin exposed the whole race of humanity to condemnation, so one act of perfect righteousness presents all humanity freely acquitted in the sight of God!")*

5:19 The disobedience of the one [1]exhibits mankind as sinners; the obedience of another exhibits mankind as righteous. *(The word, [1]kathistemi, means to cause to be, to set up, to exhibit. We were not made sinners by our own disobedience; neither were we made righteous by our own obedience.)*

5:20 The presence of the law made no difference, instead it merely highlighted the offence; but where sin increased, grace superseded it.

5:21 Death provided sin its platform and power to reign from; now grace has taken over sovereignty through righteousness to introduce unthreatened life under the Lordship of Jesus Christ over us.

A simple equation: We were not made sinners by our own disobedience; neither were we made righteous by our own obedience.

The same humanity represented in the one man Adam, is triumphantly represented in the one man Jesus Christ!

Adam's transgression no longer holds the human race hostage.

6:1 It is not possible to interpret grace as a cheap excuse to continue in sin. It sounds to some that we are saying, "Let's carry on sinning then so that grace may abound." *(In the previous chapter Paul expounds the heart of the gospel by giving us a glimpse of the far-reaching faith of God; even at the risk of being misunderstood by the legalistic mind he does not compromise the message.)*

6:2 How ridiculous is that! How can we be dead and alive to sin at the same time?

6:3 What are we saying then in baptism, if we are not declaring that we understand our union with Christ in his death?

6:4 Baptism pictures how we were co-buried together with Christ in his death; then it powerfully illustrates how in God's mind we were co-raised with Christ into a new lifestyle. *(Hosea 6:2.)*

6:5 We were like seeds planted together in the same soil, to be co-quickened to life. If we were included in his death we are equally included in his resurrection. *(2 Cor 5:14 - 17.)*

6:6 We perceive that our old lifestyle was co-crucified together with him; this concludes that the vehicle that accommodated sin in us, was scrapped and rendered entirely useless. Our slavery to sin has come to an end.

6:7 If nothing else stops you from doing something wrong, death certainly does.

6:8 Faith sees us joined in his death and alive with him in his resurrection.

6:9 It is plain for all to see that death lost its dominion over Christ in his resurrection; he need not ever die again to prove a further point.

6:10 His appointment with death was [1]once-off. As far as sin is concerned, he is dead. The reason for his death was to take away the sin of the world; his life now exhibits our union with the life of God. *(The Lamb of God took away the sin of the world; [1]efapax, once and for all, a final testimony, used of what is so done to be of perpetual validity and never needs repetition. This is the final testimony of the fact that sin's power over us is destroyed. See Hebrews 9:26, "But Jesus did not have to suffer again and again since the fall (or since the foundation) of the world; the single sacrifice of himself in the fulfillment of history now reveals how he has brought sin to nought." Thus, in this context [of everyone's appointment with death], Jesus is the ultimate sacrifice. What the first, shadow-dispensation merely prophetically pointed to, he fulfilled once and for all, when he was presented as an offering, to take upon himself the sins of the entire human race! Now, with sin no longer on the agenda, he appears a second time, out of this death, to be clearly seen in everyone's whole-hearted embrace of him as Savior! [Heb 9:28].")*

6:11 This reasoning is equally relevant to you. [1]Calculate the cross; there can only be one logical conclusion: he died your death; that means you died to sin, and are now alive to God. Sin-consciousness can never again feature in your future! You are in Christ Jesus; his Lordship is the authority of this union. *(We are not being presumptuous to reason that we are in Christ! "[1]Reckon yourselves therefore dead to sin" The word, [1]logitsomai, means to make a calculation to which there can only be one logical conclusion. [See Eph 1:4 and 1 Cor 1:30].*

"From now on, think of it this way: Sin speaks a dead language that means nothing to you; God speaks your mother tongue, and you hang on every word. You are dead to sin and alive to God. That's what Jesus did." — The Message.)

6:12 You are under no obligation to sin; it has no further rights to dominate your dead declared body. Therefore let it not entice you to obey its lusts. *(Your union with his death broke the association with sin [Col 3:3].)*

6:13 Do not let the members of your body lie around loose and unguarded in the vicinity of unrighteousness, where sin can seize it and use it as a destructive weapon against you; rather place yourself in [1]readiness to God, like someone resurrected from the dead and present your whole person as a weapon of righteousness. *(Thus you are reinforcing God's grace claim on mankind in Christ; [1]paristemi, to place in readiness, in the vicinity of.)*

6:14 Sin was your master while the law was your measure; now grace rules. *(The law revealed your slavery to sin, now grace reveals your freedom from it.)*

6:15 Being under grace and not under the law most certainly does not mean that you now have a license to sin.

6:16 As much as you once gave permission to sin to trap you in its spiral of spiritual death and enslave you to its dictates, the obedience that faith ignites now, introduces a new rule, rightness with God; to this we willingly yield ourselves. *(Righteousness represents everything that God restored us to — in Christ.)*

6:17 The content of teaching that your heart embraced has set a new [1]standard to become the [1]pattern of your life; the grace of God ended sin's dominance. *(The word, [1]tupos, means form, mold. The Doddrich translation translates it as, "the model of doctrine instructs you as in a mold.")*

6:18 Sin once called the shots; now righteousness rules.

6:19 I want to say it as plainly as possible: you willingly offered your faculties to obey sin, you stained your body with unclean acts and allowed lawlessness to gain supremacy in all of your conduct;

in exactly the same way, I now encourage you to present your faculties and person to the supremacy of righteousness to find unrestricted expression in your lifestyle.

6:20 You were sins' slaves without any obligation to righteousness.

6:21 I know you are embarrassed now about the things you used to do with your body; I mean was it worth it? What reward or return did you get but spiritual death? Sin is a cul-de-sac. *(Sin is the worst thing you can ever do with your life!)*

6:22 Consider your life now; there are no outstanding debts; you owe sin nothing! A life bonded to God yields the sacred expression of his character, and completes in your experience [1]what life was always meant to be. *(Lit. The life of the ages, [1]aionios; traditionally translated, "and the end, eternal life".)*

6:23 The reward of the law is death the gift of grace is life! The bottom line is this: sin employs you like a soldier for its cause and rewards you with death; God gifts you with the highest quality of life all wrapped up in Christ Jesus our Leader. *(A soldier puts his life on the line and all he gets in the meantime is a meager ration of dried fish for his effort! opsonion, a soldier's wage, from opsarion, a piece of dried fish.)*

7:1 I write to you in the context of your acquaintance with the law; you would agree with me that laws are only relevant in this life.

7:2 A wife is only bound by law to her husband while he lives; any further legal claim he has on her ends with his death.

7:3 The law would call her an adulteress should she give herself to another man while the first husband is still alive. Yet, once he's dead, she is free to be another's wife.

7:4 The very same finality in principle is applicable to you, my brothers and sisters. In the incarnate Christ you died to the system of the law; your inclusion in his resurrection brought about a new union. Out of this marriage, *[faith]* now bears children unto God. *(Where the first marriage produced sin [a forgotten identity]; righteousness [rediscovered sonship] is the child of the new union. In the previous chapter Paul deals with the fact that our inclusion in Christ in his death broke the association with sin; now he reveals that it also broke the association with the system of the law of works as a reference to righteousness.)*

7:5 At the time when the flesh ruled our lives, the subtle influences of sins which were ignited by the law, conceived actions within us that were consistent in character with their [1]parent and produced spiritual death. *([1]The "parent" Paul refers to is the law-system of self effort based on the fruit of the "I am not" Tree. See my notes in 1 John 3:12.)*

7:6 But now we are fully released from any further association with a life directed by the rule of the law, we are dead to that which once held us captive, free to be slaves to the newness of spirit-spontaneity rather than age old religious rituals, imitating the mere face value of the written code. *(The moment you exchange spontaneity with rules, you've lost the edge of romance.)*

7:7 The law in itself is not sinful; I am not suggesting that at all. Yet in pointing out sin, the law was in a sense the catalyst for sinful actions to manifest. Had the law not said, "Thou shall not covet," I would not have had a problem with lust.

7:8 But the commandment triggered sin into action, suddenly an array of sinful appetites were awakened in me. The law broke sin's dormancy.

7:9 Without the law I was alive; the law was introduced, sin revived and I died.

7:10 Instead of being my guide to life, the commandment proved to be a death sentence.

7:11 Sin took advantage of the law and employed the command-ment to seduce and murder me.

7:12 I stress again that the law as principle is holy and so are the ten commandments; it consistently promotes that which is just and good.

7:13 How then could I accuse something that is that good to have killed me? I say again, it was not the law, but sin that caused my spiritual death. The purpose of the law was to expose sin as the culprit. The individual commandment ultimately serves to show the exceeding extent of sin's effect on mankind.

7:14 We agree that the law is spiritual, but because I am ¹sold like a slave to sin, I am reduced to a mere carnal life. *(Spiritual death. The word, ¹**piprasko** comes from **perao**, meaning to transport into a distant land in order to sell as a slave. Sin is a foreign land.)*

7:15 This is how the sell-out to sin affects my life: I find myself doing things my conscience does not allow. My dilemma is that even though I sincerely desire to do that which is good, I don't, and the things I despise, I do.

7:16 It is obvious that my conscience sides with the law;

7:17 which confirms then that it is not really I who do these things but sin manifesting its symptoms in me. It has taken my body hostage. *(Sin is similar to a dormant virus that suddenly breaks out in very visible symptoms.)*

7:18 The total extent and ugliness of sin that inhabits me, reduced my life to good intentions that could not be followed through.

7:19 Willpower has failed me; this is how embarrassing it is, the most diligent decision that I make to do good, disappoints; the very evil I try to avoid, is what I do. *(If mere quality decisions could rescue mankind, the law would have been enough. Good intentions cannot save someone. The revelation of what happened to us in Christ's death is what brings faith into motion to liberate from within. Faith is not a decision we make to give God a chance, faith is realizing our inclusion in what happened on the Cross and in the resurrection of Christ! See Rom 3:27.)*

7:20 If I do the things I do not want to do, then it is clear that I am not evil, but that I host sin in my body against my will.

7:21 It has become a predictable principle; I desire to do well, but my mere desire cannot escape the evil presence that dictates my actions.

7:22 The real person that I am on the inside delights in the law of God. *(The law proves to be consistent with my inner make-up.)*

7:23 There is another law though, *(foreign to my design)* the law of sin, activating and enrolling the members of my body as weapons of war against the law of my mind. I am held captive like a prisoner of war in my own body.

7:24 It doesn't matter how I [1]weigh myself by my own efforts, I just do not measure up to expectations. **The situation is absolutely desperate for mankind; is there anyone who can deliver them from this death trap?** *(The word [1]talaipōros occurs only twice in the New Testament - Rom 7:24, Rev 3:17 - and both times it is translated wretched!? It has two components, **talanton**, which is the word for a scale of balance; that which is weighed, a talent [of gold]; and **poros** from **peira**, to examine closely, to pierce; a test to determine the hidden value of something. You cannot measure temperature with a ruler. See 2 Cor 3:15 In the meantime nothing seems to have changed; the same veil continues to blindfold the hearts of people whenever Moses is read. (Moses symbolizes the futility of self righteousness as the global blindfold of the religious world. [John 1:17] Against the stark backdrop of the law; with Moses representing the condemned state of mankind, Jesus Christ unveils grace and truth. He is the life of our design redeemed in human form.)*

*2 Cor 3:16 The moment anyone [1]returns to the Lord the veil is gone. (The word, [1]**epistrepho** means to return to where we've wandered from; "we all like sheep have gone astray." Jesus is God unveiled in human form. [Col 1:15] Also 1 Pet 2:25 You were completely vulnerable, just like sheep roaming astray without direction or protection, but now you have returned and are restored to the shepherd and Guardian of your souls. And 1 Pet 1:17. Then, Hebrews 8:1, "The conclusion of all that has been said points us to an exceptional Person, who towers far above the rest in the highest office of heavenly greatness. He is the executive authority of the majesty of God. 8:2 The office he now occupies is the one which the Moses-model resembled prophetically. He ministers in the holiest place in God's true tabernacle of worship. Nothing of the old man-made structure can match its perfection. Heb 8:10 Now, instead of documenting my laws on stone, I will chisel them into your mind and engrave them in your inner consciousness; it will no longer be a one-sided affair. I will be your God and you will be my people, not by compulsion but by mutual desire." See James 1:25, "Those who gaze into the mirror reflection of the face of their birth are captivated by the effect of a law that frees them from the obligation to the old written code that restricted them to their own efforts and willpower. No distraction or contradiction can dim the impact of what they see in that mirror concerning the law of perfect liberty [the law of faith] that now frees them to get on with the act of living the life [of their original design]. They find a new spontaneous lifestyle; the poetry of practical living." [The law of perfect liberty is the image and likeness of God revealed in Christ, now redeemed in human life as in a mirror.])*

7:25 Thank God, this is exactly what he has done through Jesus Christ our Leader; he has come to our rescue. I am finally freed from this conflict between the law of my mind and the law of sin in my

body. *(In the Incarnation, in a human body exactly like ours, Jesus balanced the scales. He is the true measure of the life of our design - he revealed and redeemed the image and likeness of God in us as in a mirror. See Rom 1:16,17 and 3:24 and 27.*

*Note, Paul speaks of the letter of the law in 2 Cor 3:6, which he elsewhere also calls the law of works; or the law of the flesh; or the law of sin; these will-power-driven, performance-based systems enslave the masses and are only conquered by the Agape-driven law of faith [Rom 3:27] which he also calls the law of God [Rom 7:22], in which my inner man delights and my conscience embraces. [Here in verse 25 he calls it the law of my mind]. And now two verses further, in Rom 8:2 Paul calls the same law the law of the Spirit of life in Christ - James calls it the law of **eleutherios** [liberty or spontaneity - without obligation! Js 1:25] See also its reference in Rom 6:18, Rom 6:22, Rom 8:2, Rom 8:21, Rom 8:2, Gal 2:4, Gal 5:1, Gal 5:13, 1Cor 7:39, 1Cor 10:29, 2Cor 3:17, John 8:32, John 8:36, James 2:12, 1Pet 2:16, 2Pe 2:19*

2 Cor 3:6 *... The letter [of the law] is the administration of death; it is the Spirit [of grace] that quickens life.)*

8:1 Now the decisive conclusion is this: in Christ, every bit of condemning evidence against us is canceled. *("Who walk not after the flesh but after the spirit." This sentence was not in the original text, but later copied from verse 4. The person who added this most probably felt that the fact of Paul's declaration of mankind's innocence had to be made subject again to a person's conduct. Religion under the law felt more comfortable with the condition of personal contribution rather than the conclusion of what faith reveals. The "in Christ" revelation is key to God's dealing with mankind. It is the PIN-code of the Bible. [See 1 Cor 1:30 and Eph 1:4].)*

8:2 The law of the Spirit is the liberating force of life in Christ. This leaves me with no further obligation to the law of sin and death. Spirit has superseded the sin enslaved senses as the principle law of our lives. *(The law of the spirit is righteousness by faith vs the law of personal effort and self righteousness which produces condemnation and spiritual death which is the fruit of the DIY tree.)*

8:3 The law *[of Moses - Jn 1:17]* failed to be anything more than an instruction manual; it had no power to deliver us from the strong influence of sin holding us hostage in our own bodies. God disguised himself in his Son in this very domain where sin ruled us, in flesh. The body he lived and conquered in, was no different to ours. Thus sin's authority in the human body was condemned. *(Hebrews 4:15, As High Priest he fully identifies with us in the context of our frail human life. Having subjected it to close scrutiny, he proved that the human frame was master over sin. His sympathy with us is not to be seen as excusing weaknesses that are the result of a faulty design, but rather as a trophy to mankind. He is not an example for us but of us.)*

8:4 The very righteousness promoted by the law is now realized in us. Our practical day-to-day life bears witness to spirit inspiration and not flesh domination.

8:5 Sin's symptoms are sponsored by the senses, a mind dominated by the sensual. Thoughts betray source; spirit life attracts spirit thoughts.

8:6 Thinking patterns are formed by reference; either the sensual appetites of the flesh and spiritual death, or zoe-life and total tranquillity flowing from a mind addicted to spirit *[faith]* realities.

8:7 A mind focused on flesh *(the sensual domain where sin held me captive)* is distracted from God with no inclination to his life-laws. Flesh *[self-righteousness]* and spirit *[faith righteousness]* are opposing forces. *(Flesh no longer defines you; faith does.)*

8:8 It is impossible for those immersed in flesh to at the same time [1]accommodate themselves to the opinion, desire and interest of God. *(The word ἀρέσκω [1]areskoo means to accommodate one's self to the opinions desires and interests of others.)*

8:9 But you are not ruled by flesh-consciousness, *(law of works),* **but by spirit-consciousness** *[faith],* **[1]since God's Spirit is permanently [2]at home in you. Anyone who does not [3]embrace the at-homeness of the Spirit of Christ, cannot be [4]themselves.**

([1] The conditional particle [1]eiper with the Indicative Mood [οἰκέω] assumes the fact; thus, Since...

[2] The word, οικει is the Present Active Indicative of οἰκέω [2]oikeoo, thus Holy Spirit is permanently residing within.

[3] The word [3]echo means to have in hand, to hold, in the sense of wearing like a garment, to possess in mind, to be closely joined to a person.

[4] Then, the word αὐτοῦ [4]hautou G848 contracted for G1438, heauto, reflexive relation, himself, herself, themselves. In James 1:24, "for they go away from what the mirror reveals, and immediately forget what manner of person they are." Also in Romans 1:23, "Losing sight of God, made them lose sight of who they really were. In their calculation the image and likeness of God became reduced to a corrupted and distorted pattern of themselves." See also Luke 15:17, "The prodigal son came to himself... " [same word used here, [4]heauto]. This is a very important clarification to explain why the Mirror is so different here than any other translation! Other translations use αυτου G846 which is the same spelling, but G846 is from the root, autos and not hautou [G848])

8:10 The revelation of [1]Christ in you [1]declares that your body is as good as dead to sin's demands; sin cannot find any expression in a corpse. You co-died together with him. Yet your spirit is alive because of what righteousness reveals. *(The word traditionally translated, "if" [1]de ei, as in "if Christ is in you ..." can either be a condition or a conclusion, which makes a vast difference. [1]"If God be for us" (v 31) is most certainly a conclusion of the revelation of the Gospel; all of God's action in Christ confirms the fact that he is for us and not against us. Thus, [1]"because God is for us ... " in the same context this verse reveals that Christ is in us. See Galatians 1:16, "it pleased the Father to reveal his Son in me, in order that I might proclaim him in the nations." See also Romans 10:6-8, "Righteousness by faith says ... .")*

8:11 Our union with Christ further reveals that because the same Spirit who awakened the body of Jesus from the dead inhabits us, we equally participate in his resurrection. In this act of authority whereby God raised Jesus from the dead, he co-restores your body to life by his indwelling Spirit. *(Your body need never again be an excuse for an inferior expression of the Christ-life, just as it was reckoned dead in Christ's death, it is now reckoned alive in his resurrection. See Eph 2:5.)*

8:12 We owe flesh nothing.

8:13 In the light of all this, to now continue to live under the sinful influences of the senses, is to reinstate the dominion of spiritual death.

Instead, we are indebted to now exhibit the highest expression of life inspired by the Spirit. This life demonstrates zero tolerance to the habits and sinful patterns of the flesh.

8:14 The original life of the Father revealed in his Son is the life the Spirit now ¹conducts within us. *(The word, ¹agoo, means to conduct or to lead as a shepherd leads his sheep.)*

8:15 Slavery is such a poor substitute for sonship. They are opposites; the one leads forcefully through fear while sonship responds fondly to Abba Father. We are not slaves to a cruel taskmaster but gifted with the spirit of sonship; engaging the tender affection of Papa without any reserve.

8:16 Holy Spirit ¹personally entwines our spirit; resonating ²ceaselessly within, endorsing Abba's parenthood. *(The words, αὐτὸ τὸ Πνεῦμα, with ¹auto being the reflexive Personal Pronoun Nominative - thus Holy Spirit self...*

Then, the word, συμμαρτυρεῖ ²summarturei is the Present Active tense, suggesting a seamless, ceaseless endorsement; a joint-testimony. Thus, sonship is not something we imagine, but it is the very theme of God's mystery unveiled in us! **1 John 5:9,** *If we receive the testimony of men, the testimony of God is greater.* **Heb 1:1-3.**

*The Holy Spirit endorses in us what happened to us when Jesus died and was raised [**Titus 3:7**], and now echoes from within our spirits, "Abba Father."*

There is concurrent testimony of the human spirit with God's Spirit. [Vincent]

*See **Gal 4:6** To seal our sonship God has commissioned the Spirit of sonship to resonate the Abba echo in our hearts.)*

8:17 The fact that we are God's offspring, ¹certainly also means that we are equal heirs of God. Not only is God our portion, but we are his. We are co-heirs in Christ. ²So, whatever we may suffer, at any time could never separate us from our inclusion in his sufferings. Thus, every reminder of this mystery, also reinforces the fact that ³we have been made equal participants in the glory of his resurrection. *(See Eph 1:18 "I pray that your thoughts will be flooded with light and inspired insight; that you will clearly picture his intent in identifying you in him so that you may know how precious you are to him. What God possesses in your redeemed innocence is his treasure and the glorious trophy of his inheritance. You are God's portion. You are the sum total of his assets and the measure of his wealth."*

[1] Paul uses the primary particle, μέν ¹men, truly, certainly, surely, indeed.

[2] Then, the conditional particle ²eiper with the Indicative Mood assumes the fact; So ...

*Paul is fond of compounds of **sun**, together with/in union with - three in this verse - **sunklēronomoi**, co-heirs; **sunpaschōmen**, included in his suffering; sundoxasthōmen; sharing in his glory; continuing from the previous verse, **summartureō**, bearing joint witness.*

*[3] The verb συνδοξασθωμεν [3]**sundoxasthōmen** is the Aorist Passive Subjunctive of **sundoxazō** with **hina** [purpose], late and rare, here only in N.T. The Aorist Passive Subjunctive suggests inevitable fulfillment. Therefore, our equal participation in his glory is a given.)*

8:18 Thus, my most logical conclusion is this, he has taken the sting out of our suffering; what seems burdensome at the time, becomes insignificant in comparison to the glory which is about to be [1]fully uncovered [2]in us. *(See 2 Cor 4:8,16-18. The verb, αποκαλυφθηναι is [1]the Aorist Infinitive which describes the action expressed by the verb as a completed unit with a beginning and end; to be fully uncovered. Then, the preposition εἰς [2]**eis**, points to a final conclusion - in us.)*

8:19 This reflects the deepest longing of every created being - the one event, which [1]captivates their attention. Picture creation standing on tip-toe with held breath as it were, to [2]mirror-witness for themselves, the unveiling of the sons of God; can you hear the drum roll?

*([1] The word, ἀποκαραδοκία [1]**apokaradokia**, is only used here and Phil 1:20. From ἀπό **apo**, away κάρα **kara**, the head, δοκεῖν **dokein**, to watch.*

*A watching with the head erect or outstretched. Hence, waiting in suspense. The Preposition απο **apo**, away from, implies abstraction; the attention turned from other objects.*

*[2] Then the word which I translated, to mirror-witness, απεκδεχεται [2]**apekdechetai**, which is the Present Middle Indicative, of **apodechomai** - it is the timeless Present tense and in the Middle Voice, giving a personal touch to it all; it also has a reflexive quality. The word, **apekdechomai**, means to fully embrace, from **apo**, away from [that which defined me before] and **ek**, out of, source; and **dechomai**, to take into one's hands; to accept whole heartedly.)*

8:20 Every creature became subject to a frustrating life of [1]vanity and futility, because of a [2]lost identity. Creation [3]involuntarily fell prey to a mindset [4]imposed upon everyone. Yet within this stark setting, [5]hope prevails.

*[1] The word, [1]**mataiotes** from **mataios**, describes futility; vanity.*

> *See **Eph 4:17** My most urgent appeal to you in the Lord is this: you have nothing in common with the folly of the empty-minded masses; the days of conducting your lives and affairs in a meaningless way are over. (The Gentiles, ethnos, the masses of people who are walking in the vanity of their minds.)*

*Also **1 Cor 3:20** The Lord is familiar with the unfruitful search for meaning in mankind's empty debates and dialogue. (The word, dialogismos,
translates as someone deliberating with themselves. Psalm 94:11 says,
"The Lord knows the thoughts of a person; that they are vanity." The
word, μάταιος **mataios**, translates as fruitless.)*

*Then, **Titus 3:9** Avoid confusing speculations and debates about geneal-
ogies and quarrelsome controversies about the law; it is folly to engage in
such useless conversation. It is like chewing chewing-gum that has long
lost its flavor. (The word, **mataios**, translates as folly, of no purpose, from
maten, which is the accusative case of a derivative from the base of **mas-
so**, to chew, to gnaw, like eating food with zero nutritional value.*

*[2] See my comment on **Romans 7:24** It doesn't matter how I weigh myself
by my own efforts, I just do not measure up to expectations. The situation is
absolutely desperate for mankind; is there anyone who can deliver them from
this death trap?*

*[3] The words, οὐχ ἑκοῦσα [**ouk**, not and ἑκών **hekoon**, willingly] translate, [3]involuntarily.*

*This reminds of the context of this conversation where Paul states in chapter
7 that his best intention to consistently do that which is good, fails him! Alas,
his own willpower cannot save him. This is the crux of mankind's dilemma!
The duty-driven law of performance had to be rendered redundant and entirely
useless. This is now eclipsed by the Agape-driven law of the Spirit of Christ,
unveiling mankind's redeemed innocence and freedom! Rom 3:27*

*[4] The verb, υπεταγη [4]**upetage**, is the Aorist Passive of **hupotassō**, im-
posed upon - forced into subjection. [Not by God!] See **Romans 5:12-21**
...Adam's deviation set sin into motion - what happened to mankind because
of one man, Adam, is in principle typical of what was about to happen to the
same mankind because of the one man, Jesus.*

*[5] Hope prevails! Jesus is the fulfillment of the prophetic word in **Genesis
3:15**. The seed of the woman would crush the serpent's head [Ophis- the mindset of accusation based upon the deception of an inferior identity. See my notes
on **Ophis, the old Serpent** at the end of Revelation chapter 12.])*

**8:21 With eager expectation, every creature yearns to be released
from its slavery to this [1]wearisome, perishable existence; trapped
within a fragile time frame of fading glory, into the glorious freedom of discovering their true [2]sonship. They are indeed children,
and not mere "creatures" of God.**

*([1] The word, φθορας [1]**phthoras**, from **phteiro**, means to pine or waste
away, to whither.*

*See **2 Cor 11:3** I am concerned for you that you might [1]pine away through
the illusion of separation from Christ and that, just like Eve, you might
become blurry-eyed and deceived into believing a lie about yourselves. The*

temptation was to exchange the truth about our completeness [I am] with the idea of incompleteness [I am not] and shame; thinking that perfection required your toil and all manner of wearisome labor. [The word, ¹phtei-ro, means to pine or waste away, to whither. Any idea of separation causes one to whither away in loneliness.]

See 2 Cor 3:18 ... The Spirit of the Lord engineers this radical transformation; we are led from an inferior mind-set to the revealed endorsement of our authentic identity. [Changed 'from glory to glory', apo doxes eis doxan; eis, a point reached in conclusion; apo, away from, meaning away from the glory that previously defined us, i.e. our own achievements or disappointments, to the glory of our original design that now defines us; then the word doxa, glory, translates as mindset, or opinion from dokeo, authentic, blueprint-thought. Two glories are mentioned in this chapter; the glory of the flesh, which is the veiled, fading kind represented by Moses, and the unfading, unveiled glory of God's image and likeness, mirrored in the face of Christ and now redeemed in us.

[2] Note a few verses back Rom 8:15 Slavery is such a poor substitute for sonship!

This is exactly what Jesus redeemed! He mirrors the Father's parenthood of the human race.

See Heb 1:1 Throughout ancient times God spoke in many fragments and glimpses of prophetic thought to our fathers. Now, this entire conversation has finally dawned in sonship. Suddenly, what seemed to be an ancient language falls fresh and new like the dew on the tender grass. He is the sum total of every utterance of God. He is whom the Prophets pointed to and we are his immediate audience.

Heb 1:2 In a Son, God declares the Incarnate Word to be the heir of all things. He is, after all, the author of the ages. (See John 1:2 The beginning mirrors the Word face to face with God. [The beginning declares the destiny of the Word, image and likeness would be mirrored and redeemed in incarnate human form.] Also John 1:3, All things came into being through him, and apart from him nothing that exists came into being. Sonship endorses heirship. See Heb 6:16-18.)

Heb 1:3 The Messiah-message is what has been on the tip of the Father's tongue all along. Now he is the crescendo of God's conversation with us and gives context and content to the authentic, prophetic thought. Everything that God has in mind for mankind is voiced in him. Jesus is God's language. He is the radiant and flawless mirror expression of the person of God. He makes the glorious intent of God visible and exhibits the character and every attribute of Elohim in human form. His being announces our redeemed innocence; having accomplished purification for sins, he sat down, enthroned in the boundless measure of his majesty in the right and of God as his executive authority. He is the force of the universe, upholding everything that exists. This conversation is the dynamic that sustains the entire cosmos.

Also, **Gal 4:1** *Infant heirs have no more say than a slave, even though they own everything. (The best deal the law could possibly broker confirmed mankind's slavery to sin.)*

Gal 4:2 *He would remain under domestic supervision and house rules until the date fixed by his father for his official graduation to the status of sonship.*

Gal 4:3 *This is exactly how it was with us; we were kidnapped as if in infancy and confined to that state through the law. (An inferior mindset as a result of Adam's fall.)*

Gal 4:4 *But then the day dawned; the most complete culmination of time. (Everything predicted was concluded in Christ.) The Son arrived, commissioned by the Father; his legal passport to the planet was his mother's womb. In a human body exactly like ours he lived his life subject to the same scrutiny of the law.*

Gal 4:5 *His mandate was to rescue the human race from the regime of the law of performance and announce the revelation of their true sonship in God. (Now our true state of sonship is again realized. [Jn 1:12; see Jn 1:11-14] "It was not as though he arrived on a foreign planet, he came to his own, yet his own did not recognize him. [Ps 24:1] But to everyone who realizes their association in him, convinced that he is their original life, in them he confirms that we are his offspring. These are they who discover their genesis in God beyond their natural conception. Man began in God. We are not the invention of our parents. Suddenly the invisible eternal Word takes on visible form. The Incarnation. In him, in us. The most accurate tangible display of God's eternal thought finds expression in human life. The Word became a human being; we are his address; he resides in us. He captivates our gaze. The glory we see there is not a religious replica; he is the authentic* **monogenes** *begotten only of God. In him we recognize our true beginning. The Glory that Adam lost, returns. In fullness. Only Grace can communicate truth in such complete context.)*

Gal 4:6 *To seal our sonship God has commissioned the Spirit of sonship to resonate the Abba echo in our hearts; and now, in our innermost being we recognize him as our true and very dear Father.)*

8:22 We sense a global groaning of birth pangs; witnessed throughout history until this very moment. The world is pregnant with expectation.

8:23 We ourselves echo their groaning within us while we are ready to embrace the original blueprint also of our physical stature to the full consequence of sonship. What we already now participate in as first fruits of the spirit, will bloom into a full gathering of

the harvest. *(The glorified physical body [Mt 17]. Also the full realization of everything reconciled in Christ. In James 1:18, "It was his delightful resolve to give birth to us; we were conceived by the unveiled logic of God, the Word of truth." We lead the exhibition of his handiwork, like first fruits introducing the rest of the harvest he anticipates.)*

8:24 For what we already experience confirms our hope and continues to fuel our expectation for what we still cannot see. In the final visible completeness of the harvest, hope has fulfilled its function.

8:25 In the meantime our expectation takes us beyond visual confirmation into a place of patient contentment.

8:26 Likewise, the Spirit also sighs within us with words too deep for articulation, and [1]mirrors our prayers when we struggle to find words. When we're not sure how to pray properly, Holy Spirit supersedes our clumsy efforts and [2]hits bull's-eye every time.

*([1] Again a word only Luke uses, συναντιλαμβανεται, [1]**sunantilambano-mai**, which is compounded of συν, together, αντι, against, and λαμβανομαι, to support or help, and signifies such assistance as is afforded by any two persons to each other, who mutually bear the same load or carry it between them. Adam Clark*

*[2] The Spirit υπερεντυγχανει, [2]**huperentugchano** means "to strike, hit the bulls-eye" ["spot on"]. Accordingly, it is used in classical Greek as the antonym of **harmartia** ["to miss the mark, sin" - literally, to be out of sync with one's true from.])*

8:27 He who has always known us, mirrors the mind of the Spirit within us and brings our conversation back to the point. *(See the Message Bible, "He knows us far better than we know ourselves, knows our pregnant condition, and keeps us present before God."*

*I knew you before I fashioned you in your mother's womb" [Jer 1:5]. "Then you will know, even as you have always been known." [1 Cor 13:12]. Again the word, [1]**entungchano**, which means to hit the target with an arrow or javelin. This word is often translated "intercession", yet, Holy Spirit is not trying to persuade God about us, but persuades us about the Father and the finished work of the cross!)*

8:28 Meanwhile we know that the love of God causes everything to mutually contribute to our advantage. His Master Plan is announced in our authentic identity. *(Called according to his purpose, **kaleo**, meaning to surname, to identify by name.)*

8:29 He [1]has always known us face to face, and [2]engineered us upon the mirror-horizon of his faith, to be [3]jointly fashioned in the same mold and image of his Son. We see the authentic pattern of our lives preserved in the Incarnate One. He is the firstborn from [4]the same

womb that reveals our genesis. *(The word, προεγνω [1]proegnoo, is the Aorist Active of proginoskoo, to have always been known, face to face. Then again he uses the Aorist Active Indicative προωρισεν [2]prohorisen of prohoritso, I've translated, engineered us upon the mirror-horizon of his faith. Then the adjective, συμμορφός [3]summorphos the exact same form of his image [eikon]. We come from above [See John 1:13; also John 3:3-13] We were also born anew when he was raised from the dead. [1 Peter 1:3] His resurrection co-reveals our common genesis as well as our redeemed innocence. [Rom 4:25 and Acts 17:31] No wonder then that he is not ashamed to call us his siblings. The word, [5]adelphous, with a as a connective particle and delphus, the womb. We share the same origin [Heb 2:11 eks [origin; source] henos [one] pantes [everyone], and, "In him we live and move and have our being, we are indeed his offspring." [Acts 17:28].)*

8:30 Jesus reveals that we [1]pre-existed in God; he [2]defined us. He [3]rendered us innocent and also [4]adorned us with splendor and esteem. *(The word [1]prohorisen from prohoritso, pre-defined, like when an architect draws up a detailed plan. Then [2]ekalesen from kaleo, to surname, identify by name. The verb, [3]edikaiosen is in the Aorist Active form from dikaioo, to declare righteous and innocent. All the verbs in this verse are in the Aorist tense. The Aorist presents an occurrence in summary, viewed as a whole from the outside, almost like a snapshot of the action. Also [4]edoxasen from doxazō; we have been adorned with splendor and glory. He redeemed our innocence and restored the glory we lost in Adam. See Romans 3:23, 24.)*

8:31 All these things point to one conclusion, God is for us. Who can prevail against us?

8:32 The [1]gift of his Son is the irrefutable evidence of God's heart towards us. He [2]held nothing in reserve; but freely [3]gave everything we could ever wish to have; this is what our [4]joint sonship is all about. *(The word [1]paradidomi, reflects the source of the gift, the very bosom of the Father. Without reserve, ouk [strong negative] epheisato from [2]pheidomai, means to treat leniently or sparingly. To show oneself gracious, kind, benevolent, is the word [3]charizomai. The word [4]sun (pronounced soon) suggests complete union. Everything we lost in Adam is again restored to us in Christ. Sin left mankind with an enormous shortfall; grace restores mankind to excellence. [Rom 3:21-24, 1Cor 2:7].)*

8:33 God has [1]identified us, who can disqualify us? His [2]word is our origin. No-one can point a finger; he declared us innocent. *(The word [1]kaleo, means to identify by name, to surname. The word [2]eklektos suggests that we have our origin in God's thought; from ek, source, and lego, to communicate. He has placed us beyond the reach of blame and shame, guilt and gossip.)*

8:34 What further ground can there possibly be to condemn mankind? In his death he faced our judgment; in his resurrection he

reveals our righteousness; the implications cannot be undone. He now occupies the highest seat of authority as the executive of our redemption in the throne room of God. *(See Rom 8: 1, also Rom 4:25.)*

8:35 What will it take to distance us from the love of Christ? You name any potential calamity: intense pressure of the worst possible kind, claustrophobia, persecution, destitution, loneliness, extreme exposure, life-threatening danger, or war?

8:36 Let me quote Scripture to remind you, "Because of our association with you, we were ¹reckoned as sheep to be slaughtered; we have been ²jointly slain on that day. "*(The word ¹logitsomai, to take an inventory; to conclude. The word ²thanatoumetha is only used once in this form - Paul quotes the LXX in Ps 43:23 [44:22 in Hebrew text] The Preposition meta, together with, is combined with thanatos, to kill, to emphasize the idea of our joint crucifixion. Psalm 44:22. See also Ephesians 2:5,6; 4:8,9; Hosea 6:2, "After two days he will revive us, on the third day he will raise us up. We have been co-crucified, co-raised and are now co-seated together with Christ.)*

8:37 On the contrary, in the thick of these things our triumph remains beyond dispute. His love has placed us above the reach of any onslaught.

8:38 This is my conviction; no threat whether it be in death or life; be it celestial messengers, demon powers or political principalities, nothing known to us at this time, or even in the unknown future;

8:39 no dimension of any calculation in time or space, nor any device yet to be invented, has what it takes to separate us from the love of God unveiled in our Lord, Jesus Christ.

9:1 What I am about to say is my honest persuasion; I am convinced beyond doubt of our inseparable union in Christ; my own conscience bears witness to this in the Holy Spirit.

9:2 In the light of mankind's inclusion and redeemed innocence, I feel such sorrow and painful longing for my fellow Jews. *(They are all equally included but they just do not see it!)*

9:3 If it could in any way profit them I would prefer myself to rather be excluded from the blessing of Christ. If my exclusion could possibly help them understand their inclusion, I would gladly offer my body as a sacrifice.

9:4 Sonship is the natural heritage of Israel; they historically witnessed the glory and covenants and the dramatic endorsement of the law; the prophetic rituals of worship and the Messianic promises belong to them.

9:5 They are the physical family of the Messiah. Yet he supersedes all our definitions; he is God, the [1]source of blessing and the ultimate announcement of everything good, for all ages. Amen! *(The word, [1]eulogetos, means blessed, from eulogeo, good word, good news, or "well done" announcement; normally translated, blessing. The Word of God reaches far beyond the boundaries of Israel, it includes every nation.)*

9:6 It is not as though their unbelief neutralized the Word of God in its effect; Israel is no longer restricted to a physical family and geographic location.

9:7 It is not the natural seed of Abraham that gives them their [1]identity, but Isaac, the faith-child. God said, "Your children's [1]identity is revealed in Isaac." *([Gen 21:12]; [1]kaleo, to surname, or to identify by name. Mankind's original identity was not preserved in the flesh, but in the Promise.)*

9:8 By this God clearly indicates that mankind's true spirit identity is revealed in faith and not in flesh. The Promise is the fuel of faith. *(The promise ignites faith. Faith gives substance to what hope sees.)*

9:9 Remember God's pledge, "In nine months time, Sarah shall have a son." *(Genesis 18:10, "according to the time of life, thus nine months; Galatians 4:4, Jesus is the fullness of time; the promise is a Person!)*

9:10 Rebecca and Isaac also conceived, consistent with the promise, to further prove the point of faith versus performance.

9:11 God spoke to Rebecca while the twins were still in the womb. Nothing distinguished them in terms of good looks or performance. *[Except the fact that the one would be born minutes before the other, which would give him 1st born preference, according to human tradition.]*

It was recorded to emphasize the principle of [1]faith-identity as the ultimate value above any preference according to the flesh. *(The word often translated as "election" is the word [1]ekloge, from ek, origin, source and lego from logos, the word, see Jhn 1:1,14. Faith nullifies any ground the flesh has to boast in. Rom 3:27.)*

9:12 She was told, "the elder shall serve the younger."

9:13 We would say that Esau had the raw deal; he was disliked while Jacob was favored. *(And the Lord said to her, "Two nations are in your womb, and two peoples, born of you, shall be divided; the one shall be stronger than the other; the elder shall serve the younger." [Gen 25:23].*

*The two come out of the same mold; yet they represent two types of people: one who understands his true identity by faith and one who seeks to identify himself after the flesh. Again, the law of performance versus the law of faith is emphasized in order to prepare the ground for the promise-principle. Mankind's salvation would be by promise and not by performance; i.e. it would not be a reward for good behavior. No one will be justified by the tree of the knowledge of good and evil; **poneros**, "evil," full of hardships, annoyances and labor!)*

9:14 To say that God is unfair, is to miss the point.

9:15 Moses saw the glory of God's goodness; he saw God's mercy and the kindness of his compassion. *(Even when Israel deserved his absence he promised them his presence. Moses saw the glory and goodness of God, while he hid in the cleft of the rock. [Ex 33:18, 19]. Throughout Scripture the Rock represents the blueprint of mankind's original identity [Isa 51:1, Deut 32:18, Mt 16:15-18].)*

9:16 God's mercy is not a reward for good behavior; it is not a wreath given to the fastest athlete.

9:17 God employed Pharaoh as a prophetic figure to demonstrate the drama of mankind's salvation from their slavery to an inferior identity. Scripture records God's conversation with Pharaoh, (Ex 9:16) "But to show you my power working in you, I raised you up so that my Name *(revealing mankind's authentic and original identity)* might be declared throughout all the earth." *(Mankind's identity is not in Pharaoh's claim or some political leader's influence, but in their Maker.)*

9:18 The same act of mercy that he willingly bestows on everyone, may bless the one and harden the heart of the other.

9:19 This just doesn't sound reasonable at all! What gives God the right then to still blame anyone? Who can resist his will?

9:20 Who can dispute with God? The mold dictates the shape. *(There is only one true mold of mankind's design: the image and likeness of God.)*

9:21 The Potter sets the pace; same Potter, same clay; one vessel understands its value and another not; one realizes that it is priceless, the other seems worthless to itself.

9:22 Their sense of worthlessness has labelled them for destruction, yet God's power and passion prevail in patient endurance. *(God is not schizophrenic, having to balance out a seemingly unstable character by creating a nice guy and a bad guy: one for blessing and one for wrath! He cannot be both the Author of light and darkness; there is in him no shadow of compromise or change; no inconsistency or distortion whatsoever! [Jas 1:17, 18]. Mankind deceive themselves when their knowledge of their true identity becomes blurred by the flesh. "They go away and immediately forget what manner of person they are."*

Paul's noble birth carried no further significance when he discovered his spirit identity revealed in Christ. The recorded history of Israel prepares the prophetic stage of God's dealing with global mankind. Faith and not flesh would be the medium of God's dealing with man. Flesh reduces man to the senses and the soul realm, while faith's substance reveals mankind's true spirit identity. Truth immersed in agape, ignites faith. His patience is shown in Pharaoh: "So get your livestock under roof, everything exposed in the open fields, people and animals, will die when the hail comes down." All of Pharaoh's servants who had respect for God's word got their workers and animals under cover as fast as they could, but those who didn't take God's word seriously left their workers and animals out in the field [Ex 9:19-21]. "For good news came to us just as to them; but the message which they heard did not benefit them, because it did not meet with faith in the hearers." [Heb 4:2 RSV].)

9:23 He has set the stage to exhibit the wealth of his mercy upon the vessels of value. He desires to confirm in them his original intent. *(His glory, doxa, opinion, intent.)*

9:24 Being Jewish or Gentile no longer defines us; God's faith defines us. *(He "called" us; kaleo, to identify by name, to surname.)*

9:25 Hosea voiced the heart of God when he said, "I will call a people without identity, my people, and her who was unloved, my Darling." *(Even Esau whom you said that I hated. [See v 13]. It was common among the Hebrews to use the terms "love" and "hatred" in this comparative sense, where the former implied strong positive attachment, and the latter, not positive hatred, but merely a less love, or the withholding of the expressions of affection [compare Gen 29:30-31; Lk 14:26].)*

9:26 He prophesies that the very same people who were told that they are not God's people, will be told that they are indeed the children of the living God.

9:27 Isaiah weeps for Israel: "You might feel lost in the crowd, because your numbers equal the grains of the sand of the sea, but God does not abandon the individual." Numbers do not distract God's attention from the value of the one. *("Isaiah maintained this same emphasis: If each grain of sand on the seashore were numbered and the sum* *labelled 'chosen of God,' They'd be numbers still, not names; salvation comes by individual realization. God doesn't just count us; he calls us by name. Arithmetic is not his focus." — The Message.)*

9:28 For his word will perfect his righteousness without delay; his word is poetry upon the earth. *(Jn 1:1,14; Rom 1:16,17.)*

9:29 The Lord of the ¹multitudes preserved for us a Seed, to rescue us from the destruction of Sodom and Gomorrah. *(From Hebrew, צבא tzaba (Strongs H6635), a host/mass of people. [See note on Rom 3:10] In Genesis 18, Abraham intercedes for Sodom and Gomorrah, "If there perhaps are 50 righteous people, will you save the city on their behalf?" He continues to negotiate with God, until he's down to "perhaps ten?" " ... there was none righteous, no not one ... ." The remnant represents the one Seed that would rescue the mass of mankind! In Romans 5:17, "one man's obedience and act of righteousness, surpasses the effect of a multitude of sins!" If (spiritual) death saw the gap in one sin, and grabbed the opportunity to dominate mankind in Adam, how much more may we now seize the advantage to reign in righteousness in this life through that one act of Christ, who declared us innocent by his grace. Grace is superior in authority to the transgression! The single grain of wheat did not abide alone! [See John 12:24] Romans 5:18-19 states, "The conclusion is clear: it took just one offence to condemn mankind; one act of righteousness declares the same mankind innocent! The disobedience of the one exhibits mankind as sinners; the obedience of another exhibits mankind as righteous!")*

9:30 This means that the nations that stood outside and excluded, the very Gentiles who did not pursue righteousness through religious discipline of any kind, have stumbled upon this treasure of faith.

9:31 Yet Israel who sought to achieve righteousness through keeping the law, based upon their own discipline and willpower, have failed to do so.

9:32 How did they fail? Faith seemed just too good to be true. They were more familiar and felt more comfortable with their own futile efforts than what they did with faith. Their faith identity *[reflected in Christ]* was a stone of offence.

9:33 The conclusion of the prophetic reference pointed towards the rock as the spirit identity of human life. In Messiah, God has placed his testimony of mankind's identity in front of their eyes, in Zion, the center of their religious focus, yet, blinded by their own efforts to justify themselves, they tripped over him. But those who recognized him by faith, as the Rock from which they were hewn, are freed from the shame of their sense of failure and inferiority. *(See Deuteronomy 32:18, "you have forgotten the Rock that birthed you...", and in Isaiah 51:1, "Look to the Rock from which you were hewn." It is only in* *him that mankind will discover what they are looking for. "Who is the son of man?" Mankind's physical identity is defined by their spiritual origin, the image and likeness of God, "I say you are Petros; you are Mr. Rock, a chip of the old block! [See Matthew 16:13-19]. Mankind's origin and true identity is preserved and revealed again in the Rock of ages. The term, "rock" in those days represented what we call the "hard drive" in computer language; the place where data is securely preserved for a long time. Rock fossils carry the oldest data and evidence of life. See 1 Peter 2:6.)*

10:1 God knows how my heart aches with deep and prayerful longing for Israel to realize their salvation.

10:2 I have been there myself. I know their zeal and devotion; their problem is not their passion, but their ignorance.

10:3 They are tirelessly busy with their own efforts to justify themselves while blatantly ignoring the fact that God already justified them in Christ.

10:4 Christ is the conclusion of the law, everything the law required of mankind was fulfilled in him; he thus represents the righteousness of the human race, based upon faith *[and not personal performance]*.

10:5 Moses is the voice of the law; he says that a person's life is only justified in their doing what the law requires.

10:6 Faith finds its voice in something much closer to a person than their most disciplined efforts to obey the law. Faith announces that the Messiah is no longer a distant promise; neither is he reduced to a mere historic hero. He is mankind's righteousness now! The revelation of what God accomplished in Christ, births a new conversation! The old type of guess-talk has become totally irrelevant; Christ is not hiding somewhere in the realm of heaven as a future hope; so, to continue to say, "Who will ascend into heaven, to bring Christ down", makes no sense at all! *(The nearness of the Word in incarnation-language is the new conversation! The word made flesh so that all flesh may witness the glory of God reflected in the radiance of their own illuminated understanding!)*

10:7 **Faith-conversation understands the resurrection-revelation** *(and mankind's co-inclusion in it. Hosea 6:2).* **The Messiah is not roaming around somewhere in the region of the dead. Someone asks, "Oh, but what about the pit? Where does the abyss fit into this? Who will descend into the abyss to bring Christ back from the dead?" This revelation takes the abyss out of the equation.** *(Those who deny the resurrection of Jesus would wish they could send someone down there and confirm their doubts, and bring back final proof that Jesus was not the Messiah. Faith announces a righteousness that reveals that mankind has indeed been co-raised together with Christ. See Eph 4:8 Scripture confirms that he arrested every possible threat that held mankind hostage. ["he took captivity captive"] And in his resurrection, he led us as trophies in his triumphant procession on high. Consider the genius of God, in the incarnate Christ, he repossessed what belonged to us by design, [4]in human form; this is his grace-gift to us. Eph 4:9 The fact that he ascended confirms his victorious descent into the deepest pits of human despair. See Luke 9:27 You don't have to wait till you're dead to see the kingdom of God; some of you standing here with me right now, are about to dramatically witness the kingdom of God* *with your own eyes. [The word, ὁράω* **horaoo**, *to stare; to gaze with wonder; to encounter; to see for yourselves. Then, in the next verse, [Lk 9:28], Peter James and John join Jesus in prayer on the mountain, where his appearance is spectacularly changed by the radiance of God's glory bursting through his skin; even his clothes became dazzling white like light. Then, the voice of his Father confirms that his beloved son is the conclusion of the conversation represented in both Moses, [the law] and Elijah, [the prophets] - "Hear him." - Jesus is the conversation of God - he is the Logos - See John 1:1,2,5,9 To go back to the very beginning, is to find the Word already present there; face to face with God. The Word is I am; God's eloquence echoes and concludes in him. The Word equals God. The beginning mirrors the Word face to face with God. [Nothing that is witnessed in the Word distracts from who God is. "If you have seen me, you have seen the Father."] The darkness was pierced and could not comprehend or diminish this light. A new day for mankind has come. The authentic light of life that illuminates everyone was about to dawn in the world. At the end of his life Peter reminds us that, 2 Pet 1:16 We are not con-artists, fabricating fictions and fables to add weight to our account of his majestic appearance; with our own eyes we witnessed the powerful display of the illuminate presence of Jesus the Master of the Christ-life. 2 Pet 1:17 He was spectacularly endorsed by God the Father in the highest honor and glory. God's majestic voice announced, "This is the Son of my delight; he completely pleases me."2 Pet 1:18 For John, James, and I the prophetic word is fulfilled beyond doubt; we heard this voice loud and clear from the heavenly realm while we were with Jesus in that sacred moment on the mountain. 2 Pet 1:19 For us the appearing of the Messiah is no longer a future promise but a fulfilled reality. Now it is your turn to have more than a second-hand, hearsay testimony. Take my word as one would take a lamp at night; the day is about to dawn within you, in your own understanding. When the Morning Star appears, you no longer need the lamp; this will happen shortly on the horizon of your own hearts. 2 Pet 1:20 It is most important to understand that the prophetic word recorded in Scripture does not need our interpretation or opinion to make it valid. 2 Pet 1:21 The holy men who first spoke these words of old did not invent these thoughts, they simply voiced God's oracles as they were individually inspired by the Holy Spirit.)*

10:8 Righteousness announced by God's faith, is the authentic conversation! Here, every definition of distance in time, space, or even indifference and hostility, is canceled. The word is no longer a distant prophetic pointer in the mouths of Moses and Elijah! They announced its destiny to be mirrored in the incarnation! "The Word is extremely close to you. It spills over from your heart and becomes dynamic conversation in your mouth!" (*Deut 30:11-14.*) **We publicly announce this message, since we are convinced that it belongs to everyone.** (*Lxx Greek OT -* ἔστιν σου ἐγγὺς τὸ ῥῆμα σφόδρα [**extremely near**] ἐν τῷ στόματί [**in your mouth**] σου καὶ ἐν τῇ καρδίᾳ σου [**in your heart**] καὶ ἐν ταῖς χερσίν σου [**in your hands!**])

10:9 Now your salvation is realized! Your own ¹words echo God's voice. The unveiling of the masterful act of Jesus forms the words in your mouth, inspired by the conviction in your heart that God indeed raised him from the dead. *(In his resurrection, God co-raised us [Hosea 6:2]. His resurrection declares our innocence [Rom 4:25]. Salvation is not reduced to a recipe or a "sinners prayer" formula; it is the spontaneous inevitable conversation of a persuaded heart! To confess, ¹homologeo, homo, the same thing + logeo, to say.)*

10:10 This is where believing happens spontaneously, in the heart! The revelation of mankind's redeemed righteousness ignites a new conversation, announcing salvation. *(The word pisteuetai is the impersonal construction, "it is believed"; believing takes place! [Present Passive Indicative of pisteuō] Faith is not something we "do" - faith is what happens to us when we realize what God has done for us! Isa 26:12 O LORD, you have wrought for us all our works. RSV. "Of God's doing are we in Christ!" 1 Cor 1:30. He restored us to blameless innocence! It is impossible not to boldly announce news of such global consequence [Isa 40:9])*

10:11 Scripture declares that, whosoever believes in Christ *[to be the fulfillment of the promise of God to redeem mankind]*, will ¹not be ashamed. *(See Isa 28:16. These two Hebrew words, חוש chush, to make haste, and [Isa 49:23] בוש bush, to be¹ ashamed, look and sound very similar and were obviously confused in some translations—the Septuagint [LXX], was the text that Paul was familiar with and there the Greek word, καταισχύνω kataischunō to be ashamed; thus, it was clearly translated from the word בוש bush.)*

10:12 Nothing distinguishes the Jew from the Greek when it comes to the generosity of God. He responds with equal benevolence to everyone who sees themselves identified in him. *(They realize that God defines them and not their cultural identity.)*

10:13 Salvation is to understand that every person's ¹true identity is revealed in Christ. *(Whosoever shall ¹call upon the Name of the Lord shall be saved; ¹epikaleomai, to entitle; to identify by name, to surname.)*

10:14 How is it possible to convince people of ¹their identity in him while they do not believe that he represents them? How will they believe if they remain ignorant about who they really are? How will they understand if the Good News of their inclusion is not announced? *(The word, ¹epikaleomai, traditionally translates as "to call upon," from kaleo, which literally means to surname, or to identify by name. This is also the stem in ekklesia, with ek being a Preposition that denotes origin, and kaleo. In the context of Matt 16 where Jesus introduces this word, he reveals that the son of man is indeed the son of God, "I say to you Simon, son of Jonah, you are Petros [Rock] and upon this petra I will build my ekklesia!" [See Rom 9:33])*

10:15 What gives someone the urgency to declare these things? It is recorded in prophetic Scripture, "How lovely on the mountains *(where the watchmen were stationed to witness the outcome of a war)* are the feet of them leaping with the exciting news of victory. Because of their eyewitness encounter they are qualified to run with the Gospel of peace and announce the consequent glad tidings of good things that will benefit everyone."

10:16 It is hard to imagine that there can yet be a people who struggle to hear and understand the Good News. Isaiah says, "Lord, who has believed our report?"

10:17 So, [1]this faith is [2]sourced in discerned hearing; the kind of hearing that recognizes the authentic unveiling of Christ as the [2]fountainhead of faith. *(Note, [1]this faith; see 2 Cor. 13:5, also, Eph 4:5. There is only one faith that matters - not what we, or a million others believe, but what God believes. Jesus is what God believes about you-manity. We are God's audience; Jesus is God's language. The Greek, [2]ek, is a Preposition that denotes origin; thus, faith emerges out of the word that reveals Christ. Hearing this dynamic message, both in the mouths of the prophets and now unveiled in the incarnate Christ, ignites persuasion.*

*The word [rhema] of "Christ", **not**, "of God" appears in the best manuscripts. It's not the mere quoting of the Scriptures that brings faith. It is the unveiling of Christ within, that does. See Luke 24:27 And beginning with Moses and all the prophets, he interpreted to them in all the Scriptures the things concerning himself. They later testified, "Did not our hearts ignite within us while he explained the Scriptures to us?")*

10:18 Has God not given mankind a fair chance to hear? Psalm 19 says, "His words touch the entire world like the rays of the sun; nothing is hid from its heat; yes, truly their resonance resounded in all the earth, and their voice unto the ends of the earth." *(Rom 1:19 God is not a stranger to anyone; whatever can be known of God is [1]manifest in man. God has revealed it in the very core of their being which bears witness within their own conscience. [Note Rom 2:14 & 15 ...The law is so much more than a mere written code; its presence in human conscience even in the absence of the written instruction is obvious. See also 2 Cor 4:4 & 7 and Col 1:27. Blindfold-mode does not remove the treasure from where it was hidden all along. Every time we love, encounter joy, or experience beauty, a hint of the nature of our Maker reflects within us; even in the experience of the unbeliever. In the incarnation Jesus unveils God's likeness, not his "otherness", in human form as in a mirror. The word [1]phaneros from **phaino**, means to shine like light. Col 2:9,10 "It is in Christ that God finds an accurate and complete expression of himself, in a human body. Jesus mirrors our completeness." While the expanse cannot measure or define God, his exact likeness is displayed in human form. Jesus proves that human life is tailor-made for God. See also Eph 4:8 And James 3:9 We can say beautiful things about*

God the Father but with the same mouth curse a fellow human made in his mirror likeness. The point is not what the person did to deserve the insult. The point is that people are image and likeness bearers of God by design.] **Rom 1:20** *God is on display in creation; the very fabric of visible cosmos appeals to reason. It clearly bears witness to the ever present sustaining power and intelligence of the invisible God, leaving mankind without any valid excuse to ignore him. [Psalm 19:1-4, "God's glory is on tour in the skies, God-craft on exhibit across the horizon. Madame Day holds classes every morning, Professor Night lectures each evening. Their words aren't heard, their voices aren't recorded, But their silence fills the earth: unspoken truth is spoken everywhere." The Message.])*

10:19 I cannot understand how Israel could be so blind as to miss the Messiah in their midst. First it was Moses who predicted that God would provoke them to jealousy with a mass of people who are the nobodies in their estimation; a seemingly senseless bunch of people will steal the show to the disgust of Israel. *("They have stirred me to jealousy with what is no god; they have provoked me with their idols. So I will stir them to jealousy with those who are no people; I will provoke them with a foolish nation." [Deut 32:21 RSV].)*

10:20 Then Isaiah in no uncertain terms hears God say, "I was stumbled upon by them who did not even bother to seek me, I became obvious to a people who did not pursue me."

10:21 "Yet My hands were continually hovering over Israel in broad daylight beckoning them, while their [1]unbelief and negative and [2]contradictory conversation caused them to blatantly ignore me." *(The word, [1]apetheo, [apathy] means refusal to believe; and [2]antilego means contradictory conversation. See Isa 65:1 I was ready to be sought by those who did not ask for me; I was ready to be found by those who did not seek me. I said, "Here am I, here am I," [mirror-language] to a nation that did not call on my name. Isa 65:2 I spread out my hands all the day to a rebellious people, who walk in a way that is not good, following their own devices.)*

11:1 I want to make it clear that I am not saying that God rejected Israel, my own life bears witness to that, and I am as Jewish as you can get; you can trace me back to Benjamin and Abraham.

11:2 God did not push his people aside; his reference is his knowledge of them before they rejected him. Scripture accounts occasions where God had abundant reason to abandon Israel. Elijah hits out against them and lists their sins to persuade God to utterly cast them off. (*proginosko* - *to know in advance.*)

11:3 "Lord, they butchered your Prophets, and undermined your provision through the sacrificial altar; I am the only one left and scared to death." (*1 Kings 19:14.*)

11:4 Yet God answers him in a completely different tone, "You are counting wrong, you are not alone; I have seven times a thousand on reserve who have not bowed the knee to Baal. They have not exchanged me for a foreign owner." (*Seven times a thousand refers to an innumerable amount and not to an exact 7000 people. The Hebrew word "Baal" בעל means owner, husband or master [1 Kings 19:18].*)

11:5 Thus even in today's context, God's original word of grace has preserved a remnant of much larger proportion than what we can number. (*The word, **ekloge**, from **ek**, a Preposition denoting source or origin, + **logos**, word or logic, thus translated as the "original word." Traditionally this is translated as "election."*)

11:6 Grace cannot suggest debt or obligation at the same time. The word grace can only mean what it says. The same argument goes for mankind's good works; if salvation or any advantage for that matter is to be obtained according to prescribed regulations of conduct, then that's it. No amount of grace can change the rules! Grace means grace and work means work.

11:7 The very thing Israel sought to obtain through their diligent labor they failed to get; yet those who embraced grace as God's [1]original intent hit the bull's eye every time, leaving the rest groping around in the dark like blindfolded archers. (*[1]eklego: the original reasoning, logic, word.*)

11:8 Isaiah said that God has given them a spirit of slumber, causing their eyes and ears not to function. This drowsiness seems to prevail even to this day. (*Unbelief and religious ritual are blindfolds. "And the Lord said, this people draw near to me with their mouth and honor me with their lips but remove their hearts and minds far from me, and their fear and reverence for me are a commandment of men that is learned by repetition ..." [Isa 29:10, 13].*)

11:9 David sees how the very table of blessing has become a stumbling block to them through their ignorance. The table of the Lord is the prophetic celebration of the sacrificed Lamb, where God himself provides redemption according to the promise; yet therein they were trapped and snared and they stumbled by their own unbelief. Now their only reward is the table they set for themselves. *Commentary by John Gill: "... the table may be called an altar." 'You put unclean bread on my altar. And you say, 'How have we made it unclean?' By your saying, the table of the Lord is of no value [Mal 1:7].*

The sacrifices offered up upon "the table;" their meat offerings and drink offerings, and all others, likewise the laws concerning the differences of meats and indeed the whole ceremonial law which lay in meats and drinks and such like things; now the Jews are placing their justifying righteousness before God, in the observance of these rites and ceremonies, and imagining that by these sacrifices their sins are really expiated and atoned for; they neglected and submitted not to the righteousness of Christ, but went about to establish their own so that which should have led them to Christ became a handwriting of ordinances against them, and rendered Christ of no effect to them. Moreover, the sacred writings, which are full of spiritual food and divine refreshment, the prophecies of the Old Testament which clearly pointed out Christ, are not understood but misapplied by them, and proved a trap, a snare, and a stumbling block to them.)

11:10 This is the penalty of their disbelief; eyes that constantly fail to focus on the fact that Christ took their burdens and now their backs are still bending to the point of breaking under the strain of their own burdens.

11:11 Does this mean that the Jews are beyond redemption? Is their stumbling permanent? No! May it never be too late for them. Their failure emphasized the inclusion of the Gentile nations. May it only prove to be their wake-up call.

11:12 If their stumbling enriched the rest of the world and their lack empowered the Gentiles, how much more significant will their realizing their completeness be?

11:13 In my capacity as a representative of the Good News to the Gentiles, I will speak in such a way that the clarity of my conclusion

11:14 will provoke my own flesh-and-blood family to jealousy. I know that my words will rescue many of them.

11:15 The Gentile nations realized their inclusion in Christ in a sense at the expense of the Jews; to now also embrace the Jews in the welcome of God is to raise them from the dead.

11:16 The seed sets the pace; it sanctifies what sprouts from it. Seed produces after its kind. If the invisible root is holy so are the visible branches.

11:17 And if some of the original branches were broken off, and you Gentiles like a wild olive were grafted in to partake of the same nourishing fatness of the roots,

11:18 then there is no cause for boasting against the ignorance of the Jews because you are now suddenly better off than they are. Remember, the roots sustain the branches, and not the other way round!

11:19 There is no point in thinking that in order to accommodate you, God had to first break off the Jewish branches.

11:20 Their unbelief was their loss; your faith is your gain.

11:21 God could do them no favors just because they were the natural branches; neither does God now owe you any special privileges.

11:22 Both God's goodness as well as his decisiveness are based on his integrity; unbelief is not tolerated, not in them, neither will it be tolerated in you. His favor is not to be taken for granted; instead, continue to embrace and appreciate his goodness with gratitude.

11:23 The moment Israel turns from their unbelief, God is ready to immediately graft them back into the tree.

11:24 You were cut out of the unfruitful olive tree and were grafted into the stock of the original tree. How much more will these natural branches be grafted again into their original identity.

11:25 Do not be ignorant then of the [1]mystery of their temporal exclusion; their blindness opened your eyes to the fullness of God's plan for the whole world. *(In Paul's reference to the gospel, he often uses the word mystery to emphasize the genius of God in "hiding" the treasure of the gospel from view. See 1 Corinthians 2:1-16. Also see Math 13:44, the man who found the treasure, hid it again! See Further notes on, Why the Mystery, at the end of the chapter)*

11:26 Once the nations realize the full extent of their inclusion, then all Israel shall also be saved. Just as it is written prophetically, "There shall come a Deliverer out of Zion; he shall turn ungodliness away from Jacob.

11:27 For this is my covenant with them that I shall take away their sins." *("And as a Savior he will come to Zion, turning away sin from Jacob, says the Lord." [Isa 59:20] "And as for me, this is my agreement with them, says the Lord: my spirit which is on you, and my words which I have put in your mouth will not depart from your mouth, or from the mouth of your children, or from the mouth of your children's children, says the Lord, from now and for the ages to come." [Isa 59:21].)*

11:28 In your estimation they appear to be enemies of the gospel, but their Father's love for them has not changed. He knows their original worth.

11:29 For God's grace gifts and his persuasion of mankind's original identity are irrevocable. *(kaleo - to surname, to identify by name.)*

11:30 In days gone by, you did not believe God; yet in a sense Israel's unbelief opened the door for you to realize God's mercy.

11:31 Now you are returning the favor as it were; your testimony of his mercy extends an opportunity to them to turn from their unbelief and embrace mercy.

11:32 In God's calculation the mass of mankind is trapped in unbelief. This qualifies all mankind for his mercy.

11:33 Oh, how amazing is the depth of the wealth of God's wisdom and knowledge. The understanding of his judgements can only be sourced in a conversation that originates from above; his ways are only accessible in the footprints of his thoughts. *(The word ἀνεξερεύνητος anexereunētos from ana, upward and exereunaō, to search out [1 Pet 1:10] from ek, source, and ereo, to utter to speak - [only here and in Eph 3:8] Again the next word begins with the Preposition ana - ἀνεξιχνίαστος anexichniastos from ana, upward and ek, source and ichnos, a footprint. Sadly, both these words have been wrongly translated to suggest that it is impossible to explain God's decisions or to understand his ways. Sounds like Isa 55:8,9 until verse 10 comes to the rescue. "BUT. Just as the rain and the snow come down from heaven [from above] and saturate the soil, SO shall my Word be. The Incarnation is the key to understanding God's thoughts and his ways.)*

11:34 Who inspired his thought? Who sat in council with him?

11:35 Is God indebted to anyone?

11:36 Everything originates in him; finds both its authentic expression and ultimate conclusion in him. His opinion rules the ages. We cannot but agree with our yes and awe. Amen.

Further notes on, Why the Mystery?

Romans 11:25 Do not be ignorant then of the [1]mystery of their temporal exclusion; their blindness opened your eyes to the fullness of God's plan for the whole world. *(In Paul's reference to the gospel, he often uses the word mystery to emphasize the genius of God in "hiding" the treasure of the gospel from view. See 1 Corinthians 2:1-16.*

In *Matthew 13:44*, Jesus tells one of my most favorite parables. "The kingdom of heaven is like a treasure hidden in a field, which a man found and covered up; then in his joy he went and sold all that he had and bought the entire field. *(Greek, **agros**; an agricultural field.)* The fact that it is an agricultural field means that it already has a calculated, historical value. It has been cultivated for many years and valued accordingly. But now, the presence of a hidden treasure immediately brings a new dynamic to the table - there is much more to the field than what meets the eye. Imagine how intrigued his Jewish audience was. They themselves were farmers and business men - and here's a man, who has discovered something that no one else knew about. This puts him in a most unique position to buy a farm for a ridiculous bargain. And if, in this narrative, the field represents the world, then it is in a bad shape. Overgrown with thorns and thistles, and certainly one could point to many flaws that should influence the seller to settle for a much reduced price; they must have reasoned. But, Jesus shocks them out of their wits when he reveals that the man who found the treasure hid it again, and goes away and sells all he has and buys the entire field. This doesn't make any sense. Why would this man be prepared to pay such a ridiculous and most extreme price, knowing that no one else had a clue about the treasure.? Who did he it buy from? I mean, a thief surely never gets ownership; so, God did not buy us back from no "devil". The man who discovered the treasure is also the original owner of the field. Psalm 24:1 The earth is the LORD's and the fullness thereof, the world and those who dwell therein. There is only one legitimate Father. Herein lies the crux of the story. Jesus very intentionally tells this in a language that will awaken us to the most amazing discovery about ourselves. The mystery, that was hidden for ages and generations, is unveiled. He was about to ransom us from our own ignorance; our fallen mindsets *[diabolos, thru the fall]*, and the lies we believed about ourselves. See Heb 6:17; he desired to show more convincingly to the heirs of the promise the unchangeable, non-negotiable character of his resolve - so he swore by himself. How was it possible to interpret Math 13:44 any other way? Who bought who from whom? Law-language cannot comprehend gift language. He sold all he had and bought the entire field to persuade mankind that they belonged to him all along. The "field" is all he has. God has no other interest in the universe but you. The whole of the gospel is to persuade us of our original, and now redeemed value. See 1 Peter 1:18,19.

12:1 Live consistent with [1]who you really are, inspired by the loving kindness of God. My [2]brothers, the most practical expression of worship is to [3]make your bodies available to him as a living sacrifice; this pleases him more than any religious routine. He desires to find visible, individual expression in your person. *(The word, [1]parakaleo, comes from **para**, a Preposition indicating close proximity; a thing proceeding from a sphere of union; to have sprung from its author and giver; originating from a place of intimate connection; and the word **kaleo**, meaning to identify by name, to surname. Jesus introduces the Holy Spirit in the same capacity: **parakletos**, meaning close companion, kinsman [John 14:16]. The word, [2]**adelphos**, comes from **a**, as a connective particle, and **delphos**, meaning womb. Commonly translated as brother. [See Heb 2:11] The word, [3]**paristemi**, means to exhibit, to present. In the context of the New Testament, the sacrificial system no longer involves dead animals, but living people. "You died in his death and are now alive to God" [Rom 6:11].)*

12:2 Do not allow [1]current religious tradition to mold you into its pattern of reasoning. Like an inspired artist, give attention to the detail of God's desire to find expression in you. Become acquainted with perfection. To [2]accommodate yourself to the delight and good pleasure of him will transform your thoughts afresh from within. *(The word, [1]aion, is traditionally translated as "do not be conformed to this world." Actually **aion** points to a period of time of specific influence. In the context of this writing, Paul refers to the religious traditional influence of his day. The word [2]**euarestos**, comes from **eu**, praiseworthy, well done + **arestos**, meaning to accommodate one's self to the opinions, desires, and interests of others.)*

12:3 His grace gift inspires me to say to you that your thinking must be consistent with everything that is within you according to the measure of faith that God has apportioned to every individual. [1]Let the revelation of redemption shape your thoughts. *(The word [1]sophroneo means a saved mind.)*

12:4 The parallel is clear. There are many different members in one body, yet not one competes with the other in function. Instead every individual member co-compliments the other.

12:5 In Christ, the many individuals are all part of the same body and members of one another.

12:6 Our gifts may differ in function, but his grace is the same. If it is your turn to prophesy, let faith and not a title be your inspiration.

12:7 The same goes for every aspect of ministry, whether it be serving or to give instruction,

12:8 or to just be there [1]alongside someone to remind them of their true identity; always let faith set the pace. You are [3]intertwined with your [2]gift, wrapped up in the same parcel. Lead with passion; minister mercy cheerfully. (*¹parakaleo, alongside, closest possible proximity of nearness; ²metadidomi [see note on Rom 1:11], and ³haplous from ha, a particle of union and pleko, to plait, braid or weave together. You cannot distance yourself from your giving! What God now has in us is gift wrapped to the world [Eph 4:11].)*

12:9 Love without any hidden agenda. Utterly detest evil; be glued to good.

12:10 Take tender care of one another with fondness and affection; esteem one another's unique value.

12:11 Do not allow any hesitation to interrupt the rhythm of your zeal; capture the moment; maintain the boiling-point intensity of spirit devotion to the Lord.

12:12 Delight yourself in the pleasure of ¹expectation; prayer prevails victoriously under pressure. (*¹elpis, to anticipate, usually with pleasure.*)

12:13 Purpose with resolve to treat strangers as saints; pursue and embrace them with fondness as friends on equal terms of fellowship. Make yourself useful in the most practical way possible. *(See Heb 13:2)*

12:14 Continue to speak well even if someone wants to take advantage of you; bless and do not blame when you feel exploited.

12:15 Do not merely act the role in someone else's gladness or grief; feel with them in genuine joy and compassion.

12:16 Esteem everyone with the same respect; no one is more important than the other. Associate yourself rather with the lowly than with the lofty. Do not distance yourself from others in your own mind. (*"Take a real interest in ordinary people." — JB Phillips.*)

12:17 Two wrongs do not make a right. Never retaliate; instead, cultivate the attitude to ¹anticipate only beauty and value in every person you encounter. (*¹pronoeo, to know in advance.*)

12:18 You have within you what it takes to be everyone's friend, regardless of how they treat you. *(See Romans 1:16, 17. Also Matthew 5:44, 45.)*

12:19 Do not bother yourselves to get even, dear ones. Do not let anger or irritation distract you; ¹that which we have in common with one another *(righteousness)* sets the pace. Scripture confirms that the Lord himself is the ¹revealer of righteousness. (*¹ekdikeo, from ek, a Preposition denoting origin, and dikeo, two parties finding likeness in one another. That which originates in righteousness sets the pace in every relationship. The word dike is the stem word for the word, righteousness, dikaiosune. It is interesting to note that the Greek goddess of Justice is*

*Dike [pronounced, **dikay**] and she is always pictured holding a scale of balances in her hand.)*

12:20 "If your enemy is hungry, feed him; if he is thirsty, give him something to drink." These acts of kindness will be like heaping coals of fire on his head and certainly rid him of the dross in his mind and win him as a friend. *(A refiner would melt metal in a crucible and intensify the process by heaping coals of fire on it [Prov 25:21,22]. This is good strategy; be sensitive to the needs of your enemies. God sees gold in every person. Hostility cannot hide our true value. He won us while we were hostile towards him [see also Rom 5:8, 10]. His kindness led us to the radical awakening of our minds! [Rom 2:4].)*

12:21 Do not let evil be an excuse for you to feel defeated, rather seize the opportunity to turn the situation into a victory for good.

13:1 Submit to the authorities with your whole heart. Any authority only has its relevance in God. God is a God of order.

13:2 To rebel against a God ordained structure of authority is a criminal offence.

13:3 Rulers are there to encourage good behavior and frighten off any evil intention.

13:4 They represent God's desire to protect you and to do you good. The sword they carry is not for decoration; they know how to use it against evil.

13:5 Do not let fear of punishment be your motivation, rather embrace a good conscience.

13:6 The taxes you pay is to show the government that you support what they represent on God's behalf.

13:7 Fulfill all your obligations to the government, whatever the tax is that they require of you. Give them their due honor and respect.

13:8 Remain debt free; the only thing we owe the world is our love. This is the essence of the law.

13:9 Love makes it impossible for you to commit adultery, or to kill someone, or to steal from someone, speak evil of anyone, or to covet anything that belongs to someone else. Your only option is to esteem a fellow human with equal value to yourself.

13:10 Everything love does is to the advantage of another; therefore, love is the most complete expression of what the law requires.

13:11 You must understand the urgency and context of time; it is most certainly now the hour to wake up at once out of the hypnotic state of slumber and unbelief. Salvation has come.

13:12 It was [1]night for long enough; the day has arrived. Cease immediately with any action associated with the darkness of ignorance. Clothe yourself in the radiance of light as a soldier would wear his full weaponry. *(The night is far spent, [1]prokopto, as a smith forges a piece of metal until he has hammered it into its maximum length.)*

13:13 Our lives exhibit the kind of conduct consistent with the day, in contrast to the [1]parade of the night of intoxicated licentiousness and lust, with all the quarrels and jealousy it ignites. *(The word, [1]komos, refers to a nocturnal and riotous procession of half drunken and frolicsome fellows who after supper parade through the streets with torches and music in honor of Bacchus or some other deity, and sing and play before houses of male and female friends; hence used generally to describe feasts and drinking parties that are protracted late into the night and indulge in revelry.)*

13:14 By being fully ¹clothed in Christ makes it impossible for the flesh to even imagine to find any further expression or fulfillment in lust. **Jesus is Lord of your life.** (*¹enduo, fully immersed in the consciousness of the Christ-life, as defining you.*)

14:1 [1]Welcome those who are young in their faith with warm hospitality. Avoid controversial conversation. (*[1]proslambano, to take somebody as one's companion.*)

14:2 One may feel free to eat anything, while another believes one should only eat vegetables.

14:3 By having faith to eat anything does not qualify you to judge the one who abstains; God doesn't treat the vegetarian any differently.

14:4 You are in no position to criticize the hospitality of God; he invited both to the same table and he is well capable to uphold and establish someone who still stumbles and seems weak in faith.

14:5 One person may see more religious importance in some days while another values every day the same. Let everyone come to the full conclusion of what the day means in their own understanding.

14:6 Whoever esteems the specific importance of a certain day does so to the Lord, so does he who values every day equally. One eats while another abstains; both honor God in gratitude.

14:7 No one can live or die in isolation; our life and death touch others.

14:8 Neither can our life or death distance us from him; we remain his property.

14:9 The death Jesus died and his resurrection and the conclusion of his life now in us is the only relevance of life and death.

14:10 What qualifies you to be your brother's judge? On what grounds do you condemn your brother? All of us stand in the footprint of Christ. (*We are equally represented in him.*)

14:11 The Prophet recorded what he heard God say, "My own life is the guarantee of my conviction, says the Lord, every knee shall freely bow to me in worship, and every tongue shall spontaneously [1]speak with the same certainty mirrored in me!" (*The word [1]exomologeo, from ek, source, origin, **homo**, the same and logeo, to speak, thus to speak from the same source, the same inspired persuasion, to fully agree! Paul, here quotes Isaiah 45:23 See verse 20,22,& 23 "Face me and **be** saved all the ends of the earth! [Note, 'Be saved!' Not 'become saved!'] I am God; your idols are figments of your invention and imagination!" Isa 45:23 "I have sworn by myself; the word of my mouth has begotten righteousness; this cannot be reversed!" (See Rom 1:17. The Hebrew word **Yatsa** צא can be translated, begotten like in Judges 8:30) "Every knee shall bow to me and every tongue shall echo my oath!" (Thus, speak with the same certainty sourced in me! The Hebrew word, שבע **Shaba** means to seven oneself, that is, swear - thus in the Hebrew mind, by repeating a declaration seven times one brings an end to all dispute! See Heb 6:13.16,17.) See also Phil 2:10, 11.*)

This echoes what John heard in Revelation 5:13, "Then I heard the voice of everything created in heaven, upon earth, under the earth and in the sea, all living beings in the universe, and they were singing: "To him who sits upon the throne and to the Lamb, be praise and honor, glory and might, for timeless ages!" And in Colossians 1:15-17, "Now Christ is the visible expression of the invisible God. He existed before creation began, for it was through him that everything was made, whether spiritual or material, seen or unseen. Through him, and for him, also, were created power and dominion, ownership and authority. In fact, every single thing was created through, and for him. He is both the first principle and the upholding principle of the whole scheme of creation ... ." [Phillips] Colossians 1:20, "And God purposed through him to reconcile the universe to himself, making peace through his blood, which was shed upon the Cross, in order to reconcile to himself through him all things on earth and in heaven. [Weymouth Translation] In Ephesians 1:9, 10, "For God had allowed us to know the secret of his plan, and it is this: he purposed in his sovereign will that all human history shall be consummated in Christ, that everything that exists in heaven or earth shall find its perfection and fulfillment in him." [Phillips Translation].)

14:12 Thus the logic of God will find its personal expression in every person.

14:13 There remains no further cause for judging anyone. Rather determine that you will not allow suspicion or prejudice to snare your brother into a trap.

14:14 I am completely persuaded that in the Lord Jesus nothing is unclean in itself; it only seems unclean in someone's own religious reasoning.

14:15 But to walk in love is more important than to feed your appetite with your favorite food. Much rather lose out on a meal than lose a brother for whom Christ died. I mean Jesus sacrificed his life; for you to sacrifice a meal is no big deal.

14:16 Do not let your right to eat bring shame on Christ.

14:17 God's royal dominion is not based on food and drink regulations, but righteousness, *[likeness]* friendship *[peace]* and joy in the Holy Spirit.

14:18 This is definitely a win-win situation; God is pleased and people respect you.

14:19 Pursue whatever promotes peace and mutual encouragement.

14:20 Do not let a diet issue undo the work that God has done in someone's life. All foods are good in essence; it only becomes evil if someone causes or takes offence.

14:21 For your brother's sake, in order not to offend or tempt his weakness, it is better to not eat meat or drink wine in his presence.

14:22 At the end of the day, it is your own belief that matters most before God; do what your heart approves of without allowing guilt to interfere with your joy.

14:23 Don't let principle and prejudice spoil your meals! Whatever is law- rather than faith-inspired is [1]out of sync with the celebration of life! *("Whatever is not sourced in faith is sin"* [1]*hamartia, a distorted form; out of sync.)*

15:1 We who are strong in faith are obliged to lift up those who are weak, to seek their advantage and not our own.

15:2 We are to please others and consider their good and benefit.

15:3 For Christ was not in it for himself, but for us. It is written about him, that he took the full blow of the reproach and insults directed at us.

15:4 Whatever was written about him includes and represents us. We take instruction and encouragement from his patience, while Scripture is our close companion to remind us of our true spiritual identity. We anticipate the future with delight.

15:5 God's patience and reflection of who we really are transmits in us like-mindedness toward one another according to the pattern of Christ Jesus.

15:6 The opinion of God, the Father of our Lord Jesus Christ, speaks one global language in us inspired by the same passion.

15:7 This gives us all the more reason to embrace one another in friendship with the same warmth wherewith Christ embraced us into the welcome of God.

15:8 I am convinced that the ministry of Jesus Christ was confirmation to the circumcised Jews of the truth of God's promises to their fathers.

15:9 So also will the Gentile nations glorify God for his mercy towards them. David prophesied the resonance and echo of praise in the Gentile nations who would discover their true identity in his name. *(See also Ps 22:27.)*

15:10 Again Scripture reveals in Deuteronomy 32:43 that the Gentiles will join in celebration as they too are co-revealed as his people. *(See context of Deut 32.)*

15:11 Yet again in Psalm 117:1 the Gentiles are exhorted to give God praise and to join in the global applause of all the peoples of the earth.

15:12 The Prophet Isaiah sees the root of Jesse who shall rise out of the ground where it was cut off, to reign over the Gentiles; he will win their trust. *(Isa 11:1,10)*

15:13 God who is the engineer of expectation fills you to the brim with tranquil delight. The dynamic of the Holy Spirit causes faith to exceed any possible hesitation in hope.

15:14 I am completely persuaded about you, my friends, that you are able to mutually instruct one another in the full measure of the knowledge of everything that is good in you.

15:15 God's gift of grace is the motivation of my writing to you; I urge you to remember your [1]allotted portion in life. *(The word, [1]meros, means form or allotted portion; note the word translated as "sin" is ham-eros, which means to be without form, without your allotted portion. Every sin springs thus from someone's sense of unfulfillment and lack, due to ignorance concerning those things which rightfully belong to them, their true spiritual identity, their redeemed innocence, and their participating in the Divine nature which is their inheritance in Christ.)*

15:16 It is because of Jesus Christ that I am in the people business. I occupy this priestly office representing the goodness of God to [1]the masses of mankind persuading them to see how presentable and approved they are to God in the Holy Spirit. *(The word [1]ethnos, means the masses of non-Jewish people, gentiles.)*

15:17 Because of who I am in Christ Jesus, I have taken a bold stand before God.

15:18 I could entertain you with all the details of my personal adventures, yet all I desire to communicate is how actively Christ worked through my words to grab the attention of the nations.

15:19 The message was confirmed in every sign and miracle in the power of the Holy Spirit. Thus, I went full circle from Jerusalem to Illyricum proclaiming the glad tidings of Christ in its most complete context. *(Taking Jerusalem as a center, Paul preached not only in Damascus and Arabia, but in Syria, in Asia Minor, in all of Greece, in the Grecian Islands, and in Thessaly and Macedonia. Illyricum was a country of Europe extending from the Adriatic Gulf to Pannonia; it extended from the river Arsia to the river Drinius thus including Liburnia on the west and Dalmatia on the east. It now forms part of Croatia, Bosnia, Istria, and Slavonia.)*

15:20 I have placed such fond value on the fact that I could pioneer the glad tidings in many of these areas without building on someone else's interpretation of Christ.

15:21 Isaiah prophesied that, "Those who have never been told about him, will be startled to see him clearly; even though they have never heard of him, they will understand his message." *(The message of truth speaks a global language. Paul says that the open statement of the truth, which is the Word made flesh in us in the mirror reflection of Christ, appeals to everyone's conscience [2 Cor 4:2]. "Our lives are letters known and read by all." [2 Cor 3:2].)*

15:22 Now you know why it took me so long to finally get to you.

15:23 There seems to be no more room for pioneering work in these regions, after these many years I can finally fulfill my dream.

15:24 I purpose to journey all the way through Italy to Spain, but it is with great delight that I look forward to meeting with you first and enjoy a rich measure of fellowship that will again propel me onward.

15:25 I am on my way to Jerusalem to encourage the saints.

15:26 The believers in Greece, all the way from Macedonia as well as those in Achaia, have prepared a gift with great delight to bring relief to their Jewish friends in Jerusalem who are struggling financially.

15:27 They feel indebted to them since they share freely in their spiritual wealth.

15:28 As soon as I have delivered their harvest officially, I will depart to Spain via you.

15:29 I know that my coming to you will be like a cargo ship [1]filled to the brim with the blessing of everything that the Gospel of Christ communicates. (*[1]pleroma means those things wherewith a ship is filled, freight, merchandise, etc.*)

15:30 Being co-identified with you as members of a godly family through our Lord Jesus Christ and feeling the same spiritual love-bond toward one another, we are prayer partners before God joined in urgent passion.

15:31 Labor fervently in prayer with me that I will be rescued from the unbelievers in Judea, and also that my service to the saints in Jerusalem will be favorably received.

15:32 Through the pleasure of God's purpose I will arrive in Rome in joy so that we may be mutually refreshed in one another's company.

15:33 God who sustains us in oneness and [1]peace is with everyone of you. Amen. (*The word, [1]eirene, means peace, from **eiro**, to join, to be set at one again, in carpentry it is the strongest joint,referred to as the dove-tail joint.*)

The names of 37 individual believers are personally honored in this chapter of salutation. Seven home churches are also specifically mentioned, five in Rome and two in Corinth. Since Paul never visited Rome before, these people were all acquaintances, converts, fellow prisoners, or travel companions of his before they moved to Rome.

Since Prisca and Aquilla originally came from Rome [Acts 18:2, 26 and 1 Cor 16:19], they possibly purposefully returned there to start or strengthen the ekklesia together with a strong team of believers. Their strategy was to scatter several home-fellowships throughout the city. This is reflected in Paul's letter to the Corinthians where he says, "Our expectation is that as your faith increases, our field amongst you will be greatly enlarged so that we may preach the gospel also in lands beyond you." 2 Cor 10:15, 16.)

16:1 I would like to introduce Phoebe to you, she is our sister and serves the ekklesia in Corinth located in the port of Cenchreae.

16:2 Welcome her with appropriate saintly hospitality in the Lord. Support her and her business in every possible way you can. I am one of many who have greatly benefitted from her care and practical help.

16:3 Warmly embrace Prisca and Aquilla, my business partners in the Lord.

16:4 They are respected in all the Gentile churches for their unselfish lives. They have risked their own necks for me.

16:5 Salute the ekklesia in their house. Give my dear friend Epaenetus a warm hug from me. He represents the whole of Asia to me since he was my first convert there.

16:6 Miriam must also be mentioned; I remember how relentlessly she exhausted herself for others.

16:7 Embrace my cousins Andronicus and June who were in prison with me. I hold them in high regard as ambassadors for Christ; they are my seniors in him.

16:8 Hug Amliatus, my lovely friend in the Lord.

16:9 Then there is Urbanos, my co-worker in Christ, as well as my dear friend Stachys.

16:10 Acknowledge Apelles, a true veteran in Christ; honor the household of believers in the home of Aristobulus.

16:11 Say a big hello to cousin Herodian; greet the believers in the Narcissus home.

16:12 Salute Tryphena and Tryphosa whose work in the Lord bears testimony to their diligence; also my dear friend Persis who works so tirelessly.

16:13 I also remember Rufus as an outstanding worker in the Lord, and salute his mother who has become a mother to me.

16:14 I embrace Asyncritus, Phlegon, Herman, Patrobas, Hermes and all the family in fellowship with them.

16:15 Warmly greet Philologus and Julia, Nereus and his sister, as well as Olympas and all the saints in their fellowship.

16:16 Our friendship is sacred. The ekklesia of Christ here in Corinth salutes you.

16:17 Consistent with who you really are my friends, be alert to avoid anything that causes disunion or offence, contrary to the teaching that you have become acquainted with. *(Gal 1:7 There is no other gospel in spite of the many so-called Christian products branded "gospel." If any hint of the law remains, it is not good news but merely religious people's ideas, detracting from the gospel of Christ. [Some seek to unsettle your minds by perverting the Gospel to accommodate their own opinion.])*

16:18 For there are those who are not addicted to our Lord Jesus Christ but, prompted rather by the hidden agenda of their own fleshly appetites, they use their clever manipulation of words and eloquent speech to deceive the emotionally unstable.

16:19 Your ¹obedience *[faith-focus]* has become known everywhere. I am so happy for you; still, I desire for you to be wisely and exclusively acquainted with that which is good and ²innocent *[unmixed]* of evil. *(Paul's mission is to bring about the obedience prompted by faith [Rom 1:5, 16:26]. The word, ¹upoakouo, is translated as obedience or accurate hearing; and ²akeraios as unmixed, innocent.)*

16:20 God who is the author of our peace shall quickly and utterly trample ¹Satan, doing it with your feet. Your victory is realized in the revelation of the grace of our Lord Jesus Christ, and echoed *[personalized]* in your amen. *(We are the body of Christ. God desires to demonstrate his reign of peace in us by confirming satan's defeat in our practical day to day experience. The defeat of ¹accusation is celebrated in what grace communicates. The word, ¹satanas, means accuser. The law of faith defeated the law of works!)*

16:21 Timothy my co-laborer greets you affectionately; also Luke, and Jason and Sosipater who are fellow Jews, salute you kindly.

16:22 I, Tertius, who wrote this epistle, acknowledge you in the Lord.

16:23 My host, Gaius, in whose house the church meets, sends you his greetings. Then there is Erastus, the city chief who greets you, so does **Brother Quartos.** *(See Acts 19:29: Gaius was a travel companion of Paul, and he also mentions him in 1 Cor 1:14.)*

16:24 The grace of our Lord Jesus Christ belongs to you.

16:25 I am not talking "hear-say-theory"; I own the gospel I proclaim! This is my message! I salute God who empowers you dynamically and establishes you to be strong and immovable in the face of contradiction. Jesus Christ is the disclosure of the very mystery that was concealed in silence before [1]time or human [2]history were recorded. *(Titus 1:2 This is the life of the ages which was anticipated for generations; the life of our original design announced by the infallible resolve of God before [2]time or space existed. [Mankind's union with God is the original thought that inspired creation. The word, [2]**aionios**, speaks of ages.] Paul speaks of God's mind made up about us, before the ages, which is a concept in which eternity is divided up into various periods, the shorter of which are comprehended in the longer. The word, [1]**xronos**, means a measured duration or length of time; [**kairos** is a due, or specific moment of time.] This was before the ages or any measure of calendar time existed, before the creation of the galaxies and constellations. There exists a greater dimension to eternity than what we are capable of defining within the confines of space and time! God's faith anticipated the exact moment of our redeemed union with him for all eternity! "This life was made certain before eternal time." [BBE 1949, Bible in Basic English] Paul's gospel does not merely proclaim Christ in history; he announces Christ unveiled in human life; Christ in you! Colossians 1:27.)*

16:26 The mystery mirrored in [1]prophetic Scripture is now unveiled. The God of the ages determined to make this mystery known in such a way that all the nations of the earth will hear and realize the [2]lifestyle that faith ignites. *(This gospel breaks the silence of the ages and reveals how God succeeded to redeem his image and likeness in mankind. [1]Isa 53:4, 5. See note on 16:19, Faith inspires an [2]obedience of spontaneity beyond guilt and obligation.)*

16:27 Jesus Christ [1]uniquely [2]articulates the [3]wisdom of God; he is the [4]conclusion of the ages. *(Uniquely, [1]**monos**, alone, Jesus has no competition; this one man represents the entire human race; this is the mystery of the ages. 1 Cor 2:7 We voice words of wisdom that were hidden in silence for timeless ages; a mystery unfolding God's Masterful plan whereby he would redeem his glory in man. Our glorification has always been God's agenda, even before time was. 1 Cor 2:8 Neither the politicians nor the theologians of the day had a clue about this mystery [of mankind's association in Christ]; if they did, they would never have crucified the Lord whose death redeemed our glory! The word, [3]**sophos**, means clarity, wisdom. He forever broke the silence of the ages! The words, [4]**eis aion**, eis indicates a point reached in conclusion, thus the conclusion of the ages. He is the [2]**doxa**, opinion; the logos that was before time was; the Word that became flesh and dwells within us [Jn 1:1, 14]. The incarnation [Latin, **in carne**, in the body] is the final trophy of the eternal logos and doxa of God.*

Col 1:15 In him the image and likeness of God is made visible in human life in order that everyone may recognize their true origin in him. He is the firstborn of every creature. [What darkness veiled from us he unveiled. In him we clearly see the mirror reflection of our original life. The Son of his love gives accurate evidence of his image in human form. God can never again be invisible!]

Col 2:3 In Christ the complete treasure of all wisdom and knowledge is sourced.

Col 2:9 It is in Christ that God finds an accurate and complete expression of himself, in a human body! [While the expanse cannot measure or define God, his exact likeness is displayed in human form. Jesus proves that human life is tailor-made for God!]

Col 2:10 Jesus mirrors our completeness and endorses our true identity. He is "I am" in us. The days are over where our lives were dictated to under the rule of the law of performance and an inferior identity. [See Col 1:19] The full measure of everything God has in mind for a person, indwells him.)

Paul's persuasion is firmly founded in his understanding of the success of the cross. In the economy of God, Jesus represents the human race. Every possible contradiction is filtered through this perspective.

In this letter Paul addresses several concerns regarding reports of divisions amongst the believers, a sexual scandal in their ranks and questions regarding marriage, diets and money.

In the first four chapters he takes his time to reinforce their faith in the finished work of the cross as the only valid reference to their lives.

In chapters 12 and 14, he brings clarity regarding the charismatic gifts.

Then he highlights the essence of the gospel in the most beautiful love poem in chapter 13. For many years this chapter was read and preached in a typical window-shopping frame of mind.

In Paul's gospel this mindset is completely reversed; he proclaims that what God has done in Christ actually unveils the life of our design. Love celebrates the completeness of all that God has always had in mind for us. Love is not some prize one has to labor for; love mirrors who you are! What we perceived in prophetic glimpses is now concluded in completeness! (1 Cor 13:9, 10.)

In chapter 15, he emphasizes that the resurrection revelation is the theme and conclusion of the message he preaches.

Then he concludes in chapter 16:14 with, "Agape is your genesis. Loving everyone around you is what you are all about." (Our love for one another is awakened by God's love for us.) And in verse 22, he makes this final powerful statement: "Anyone who prefers the law above grace remains under the curse mentality. Jesus Christ has come; grace is the authority of his Lordship; we are so fond of him! He is the Messiah the world has been waiting for. *[The Aramaic word,* **maranatha,** מרן אתא **maran ata,** *means, "Our Lord has come"!]*)

Lydia and Francois met on the 25th of August 1974, while he was working with Youth For Christ. She was sixteen and he, nineteen. The following year he studied Greek and Hebrew at the University of Pretoria for three years while Lydia completed her nursing training. In 1978 Francois also spent a year with YWAM.

They married in January 1979 and are blessed with four amazing children, Renaldo, Tehilla, Christo and Stefan; also, three darling grandchildren Nicola and Christiaan. And 3 month old Lydie-Anne, daughter of our youngest son, Stefan and Yaël. With Christo and Keryn's Sadie arriving in July 2021.

They pioneered and worked in full-time mission for fourteen years, during which time they also pastored a church and led a training facility for more than 700 students over a five-year period. During this time he translated several of the Pauline Epistles [The Ruach Translation], which were never published; although printed along with other booklets he wrote and distributed amongst their students.

They then left the ministry and for ten years did business mainly in the tourism industry.

They built and managed a Safari Lodge in the Sabi Sand Game Reserve and eventually relocated to Hermanus where they started Southern Right Charters boat-based whale watching.

In December 2000 Francois began to write the book, "God believes in You" which led to him being invited to speak at various Christian camps and churches. Since February 2004, they travelled regularly abroad and into Africa as well as South Africa.

Francois has written several books in both English and Afrikaans, including God Believes in You, Divine Embrace, The Logic of His Love; these are also available on Kindle. Also, The Mystery Revealed and Done, which are no longer in print - although still available in Afrikaans.

In order to focus their time on writing and translation, they relocated from Hermanus in 2015, to a remote farm in the Swartberg Mountains. They have since, also stopped most of their travelling.

Lydia has written 6 amazing children's stories of which Stella's Secret, The Little Bear And The Mirror, Kaa of the Great Kalahari as well as The Eagle Story, are already published in print and on Kindle. Her most recent story "King Solitaire's Banquet" was released in December '20.

Francois passionately continues his translation of the Mirror Bible, which will eventually include the entire NT as well as select portions of the Old. The 1st 250 page, A5 edition, was published in 2012. The 10th edition Mirror Study Bible is a 7 x 10 inch book, of 1144 pages, released in April 2021.

Lydia's books are already available in English Afrikaans, German and Spanish. The Mirror Bible is currently available in Spanish, Shona, Xhosa and large portions in German.

BIOGRAPHICAL NOTE

More than 50000 people subscribe to their daily posts on Social Media; Lydia has her own fb page and Francois has 4 English pages and an Afrikaans, Spanish, Hungarian, French and Dutch page on Facebook.

Their email address is info@mirrorword.net

You can get more detail about them on www.mirrorword.net

The Mirror Bible is also on Kindle as well as an App, app.mirrorword.net

There are many of Francois' teachings on YouTube but they recently started their own

Mirror Word YOUTUBE channel, *https://m.youtube.com/channel/UC63YHk-pabON9nHgQqWeIPkA/videos*

Mirror Word PODCAST *https://open.spotify.com/show/3qsgRsf2SNDx1bubxng-w0W?fbclid=IwAR0zLo_wkVymqouQA3CvYxZ3lINrK-zUyXf4PuCql7bG-OGns-4BTcgAgRLQ*

REFERENCES and RESOURCES

Referred to by the author's name or by some abridgement of the title.

Adam Clarke (1762–1832 A British Methodist theologian)

Ackerman *[Christian Element in Plato]*

Bruce Metzger *(Textual Commentary on the Greek NT)*

Barnes Notes (Notes on the Bible, by Albert Barnes, [1834], at sacred-texts.com)

BBE (1949, Bible in Basic English)

Doddrich (Philip Doddridge 1702-1751 www.ccel.org/d/doddridge)

Dr. Robinson (Greek Lexicon by Edward Robinson1851)

E-Sword by Rick Meyers (www.e-sword.net)

J.H. Thayer (Greek-English Lexicon of the New Teatament By Joseph Henry Thayer, DD - Edinburgh - T&T CLARK - Fourth Edition 1901)

J.B. Phillips Translation (Geoffrey Bles London 1960)

Jeff Benner http://www.ancient-hebrew.org/

KJV (King James Version - In 1604, King James I of England authorized that a new translation of the Bible into English. It was finished in 1611)

Knox Translation (Translated from the Vulgate Latin by Ronald Knox Published in London by Burns Oates and Washbourne Ltd. 1945)

Marvin R. Vincent (1834-1922) Word Studies.

NEB (New English Bible New Testament - Oxford & Cambridge University Press 1961)

Robert Charles *R. H. (Robert Henry), 1855-1931*

RSV (The Revised Standard Version is an authorized revision of the American Standard Version, published in 1901, which was a revision of the King James Version, published in 1611.)

Strongs (James Strong - Dictionary of the Bible)

The Message (Eugene H. Peterson Nav Press Publishing Group)

Walter Bauer (Greek English Lexicon - a translation of Walter Bauer's Griechisch-Deutches Worterbuch by Arndt and Gingrich 1958)

Wesley J. Perschbacher (The New Analytical Greek Lexicon Copyright 1990 by Hendrickson Publishers, Inc)

Westcott and Hort *The New Testament in the Original Greek 1881*

Weymouth New Testament *(M.A., D.Lit. 1822-1902)*

Zodhiates Complete Word Study Lexicon Mantis Bible Study for Apple

NOTES

www.ingramcontent.com/pod-product-compliance
Lightning Source LLC
La Vergne TN
LVHW051352080426
835509LV00020BB/3402